# THACHERS

*island of the twin lights*

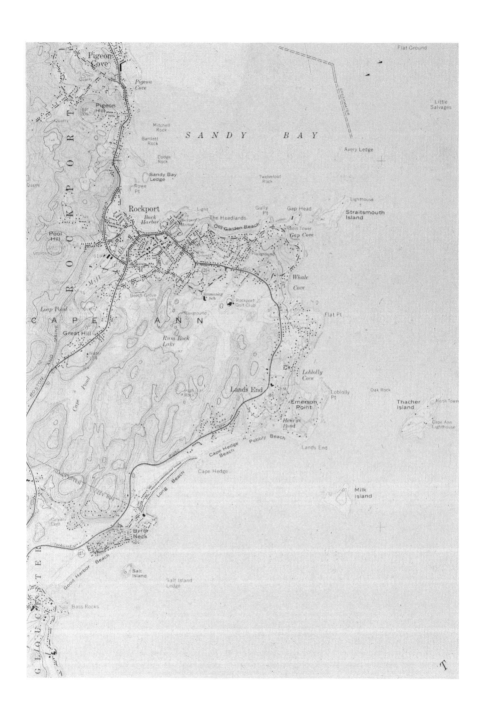

# THACHERS

## *island of the twin lights*

*by*
Eleanor C. Parsons

PHOENIX PUBLISHING
*Canaan, New Hampshire*

PERMISSION

The drawing reproduced on page 26 is from *America's Lighthouses* by Francis Ross Holland, published by the Stephen Greene Press, a wholly owned subsidiary of Viking Penguin Inc. Copyright © 1972 by Francis Ross Holland. Reprinted by permission of Viking Penguin Inc.

Parsons, Eleanor C., 1915-
  Thachers: island of the twin lights.

  Bibliography: p. 136
  Includes index.
  1. Cape Ann Light Station (Thacher Island, Mass.) —
History. 2. Thacher Island (Mass.) — History. I. Title.
VK1025.C23P37      1985          387.1'55          85-9544
ISBN 0-914659-14-6

Printed in the United States of America

# CONTENTS

Foreword                          vii

Chapter   1  /  1635-1771           1

           2  /  1771-1784         15

           3  /  1784-1814         23

           4  /  1814-1828         29

           5  /  1828-1849         32

           6  /  1849-1853         42

           7  /  1853-1860         47

           8  /  1860-1868         57

           9  /  1868-1902         66

          10  /  1893-1902         72

          11  /  1902-1908         78

          12  /  1908-1919         84

          13  /  1919-1930         90

          14  /  1930-1933         94

          15  /  1933-1939        100

          16  /  1939-1967        104

          17  /  1967             112

          18  /  1967-1980        115

          19  /  1980-1981        122

          20  /  1981-1982        128

Appendices

    Bibliography                 136

    Lighthouse Keepers           137

    Illustrations & Credits      138

    Index                        140

# FOREWORD

*M*UCH OF MY WRITING has been in the field of regional history but why, you may ask, would anyone choose to write about an island only half a mile long, a quarter mile wide, and covered with rocks, brier and poison ivy?

About five years ago Thacher Island was named to the National Registry of Historic Places and, while never minimizing the island's long history of life-saving, this gave the island a new importance as a miniature national park. As a result of renewed public interest and curiosity, I began to research this island's past.

Rockport town hall records turned up Thatcher Warren Kezer, the single person still living who was actually born on the island. I consulted local librarians, the Coast Guard Academy at New London, and the Coast Guard records in the Washington, D. C. archives. Immediately it became evident that, instead of one story, there were five major stories to be developed:

> The story of the Anthony Thacher shipwreck
> The building of the twin stone towers
> The evolution of the lights
> The lightkeepers and their families
> The shipwrecks in the vicinity of the island.

In order to keep on track, I made a chronological table of events covering 350 years, and another chronological table for the evolution of the lights from candle to whale oil to the present unmanned, computerized light. By this time I was hooked on my subject.

I joined the new Thacher Island Association and took my first boat trip to the island, savored a clambake on the island and examined seagull eggs. I ascended both north and south towers, at the expense of sore muscles, counting the 148 steps in each as I climbed. I followed the cleared trail all the way around the island trying to determine the exact location of Anthony Thacher's shipwreck. I absorbed sea smells and sea sounds, studied wind, current, and shoreline, then looked back toward the mainland and tried to feel as the lightkeepers and their families must have felt in their isolation there.

Help now appeared from unexpected sources, and many people offered photographs, anecdotes, and even their personal diaries. Among those to whom I am indebted are: Cora Seavey Sweet who grew up on the island; Brother David Cook, of the Order of LaSalette Shrine, for his extensive family records and photographs of his grandfather, John Cook; Esther Johnson and her daughter, Connie Spiewak, for news clips and biographical data; Charlotte Hatfield of Chebeague Island, Maine; Francis and Gladys Haskell for information and anecdotes; Dina Hamilton, Alice Mills Gray, Alice Reed Brown, Louise Reed Leslie, Helen Towle, Virginia Eddy, Nancy Lee Gray; and for photographs, Phil Bissell, Rosemary Lesch, Gary Taber, and the *Gloucester Daily Times*.

The departure of Russell Grubb as first keeper under the new program of restoration concluded the story. Therefore the appointment of the present island keeper, Harold Whitaker, and his wife, Sylvia, as well as details of the great storm damage to the boat ramp in 1984, are not included. Nevertheless, help from the Whitakers has been ongoing and much appreciated.

A special thanks must go to my daughter, Rosemary Lesch, a charter member of the Thacher Island Committee, member of the clean-up crew for the north tower, and my consultant in matters pertaining to the island. As a trained assistant to the Rockport Harbor Master her knowledge of area tides, currents, and the restoration program has been an invaluable source of information.

The help and encouragement of so many have made possible the publication of the book to coincide with the 350th anniversary date of the Anthony Thacher shipwreck of August 14, 1635.

Eleanor C. Parsons

Rockport, Massachusetts
March 15, 1985

# THACHERS

*island of the twin lights*

## 1635–1771

*U*P TO OUR MIDDLES in salt water we sat." This single line could have been spoken by any one of thousands of shipwrecked sailors and gone unremembered. Instead, the nine sober, impassive words, preserved in a letter more than 300 years old, recall for us one of the great tragedies of the New England coast, a tragedy so overwhelming with grief that each time the story is told it has the power to wring the heart of the listener.

This sorrowful event of August 14, 1635, with the loss of twenty-one lives, was the earliest shipwreck known to have occurred along the New England coast. But, "with every given life comes a new life," and a new life was given to the island near which the shipwreck occurred.

Imagine an island with more than 50 acres of boulder and brier; then build on these acres identical twin towers of stone that thrust 124 feet skyward and look like twin turrets of some enchanted castle. Add a half-dozen lesser buildings of assorted sizes and shapes and a couple of thousand sea gulls. Surround it with the Atlantic Ocean, concealing, as it does, the splintered remnants of countless wrecked vessels, and at this first fleeting glance you have Thachers Island—but this is an illusion. There is much more than first meets the eye.

This island, located off the Massachusetts coast and recently listed in The Register of Historic Places, is owned by the United States government, but it "belongs" to Rockport, and it is the people of Rockport and all the Cape Ann communities, as well as visitors who cherish this now famous island.

1

What makes a historic landmark? What brings such fame to a barren island, one of a half million islands scattered about the world, that it is important to preserve it for future generations? Its age? Famous people? A parade of exciting events? Or is it some mysterious quality more compelling than all these?

For Thachers Island there is no question of age, for it traces its ancestry back thousands of years to the Age of Ice. Perhaps, though, doubts may linger about its "famous" people, for it is known that no more than five families ever lived on this island at any one time. Nevertheless, as we shall see, a constant stream of people, many of them ordinary working men and women, have shaped the story of this island in a remarkable way.

But how can an island of boulder and brush claim a parade of exciting events? This island provides no soft music, no glamorous evening parties, no luxury hotels. Its music has always been the rhythmic roar of surf on rock. In early times, the parties were most often the night watch and the filling of oil containers to keep the lights aglow. Then, the hotels were the three modest dwellings with angular ells and the red brick, the gray stone, the salt-washed whiteness characteristic of New England architecture.

Thachers Island is assaulted by snowstorms in winter, by electrical storms in summer, and by countless numbers of nor'easters all year round. There have been so many shipwrecks on the island that sailors have long considered it one of the most hazardous places along the Atlantic coast. It has known many acts of heroism involving the loss of life and the saving of lives — these, too, uncounted — and once in a dense fog it prevented the death or injury of a United States president.

Besides being witness to heroism, to birth, life, and death, it has observed scientific experiments, inventions, experimental farming. It has witnessed, too, the laying of a transatlantic cable along the floor of the ocean and construction of a breakwater designed to rise above the ocean's surface and to cover 1,377 acres.

In addition to these events, political intrigue found its way to this island more than once, creating a stir on both island and mainland. In more recent years, to the dismay of many on the mainland, it sheltered a criminal while he was being held in protective custody by federal authorities; and, according to one woman who lived there for a time, it has been the cause of divorces.

All these events share in the Thachers Island story, but it was a single incident that brought this now famous island to prominence and established the course that was to make it a historic landmark. Though the tragedy occurred 350 years ago, details of its story so thoroughly imprinted themselves on the minds of New Englanders that it was as if the words of the story were actually carved in the stone towers of the island.

Although the island was not yet named at the time of this tragedy, it was not entirely unknown, for some twenty years earlier explorers had observed it with interest. Champlain had circled it at one time, and twenty years later Capt. John Smith included it as the largest of three islands that he called the Turks' Heads.

The island, until then nameless and scarcely known, sat in a kind of forlorn splendor amid the crashing waves just off the southeastern point of Cape Ann — too far to reach by swimming, yet too near to ignore its presence. For this island has a presence not unlike that of an actor when he appears onstage, and after that gale-driven August day it became a presence not easily ignored. This hitherto undiscovered island at once became the talk of all New England, and the name of the man who sat up to his middle in salt water has been perpetuated in history and poetry and song.

Anthony Thacher was an Englishman who had recently come from London, with a name as little known in America as the island itself, and the name of his wrecked vessel — prophetic for the island it was to bring to prominence — was the *Watch and Wait*.

By the time the shipwreck of the *Watch and Wait* took place, a shipping lane had already been established to pass by the island. Some Indians from the mainland had probably scouted the island as well; later years were to bring fishermen, soldiers, pirates, farmers, lighthouse keepers, inventors, and even criminals. For purposes of history, however, the island began in 1635 with Anthony Thacher's tragedy, when the island acquired a name.

"Thacher's Woe," he moaned in his profound grief, and the island became his own. Indeed, the island was literally his when, a few months after the shipwreck, a generous and compassionate Massachusetts General Court gave the island to him for whatever use he could make of it. The island was then said to contain about eighty acres, some of it suitable for pasturage but much of it craggy, barren rock. The island must have seemed an ironic gift to Anthony Thacher, who probably would have wished for nothing more than to erase from his mind the memory of that tragic day.

The storm that wrecked the *Watch and Wait* had been going on for over a week. Early in the week the wind had shifted from southeast to south-southeast to northeast. Seas were running heavy, and roaring tides pounded the shore. Naturally, there was apprehension about the weather,

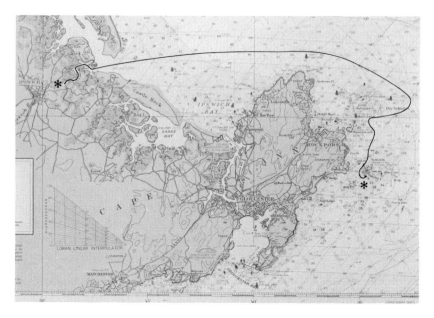

Route of the *Watch and Wait* from Ipswich to its wreck on the southerly shore of Thachers Island in 1635, superimposed on a section of a USGS Rockport quadrangle.

but the *Watch and Wait* resolutely kept to its schedule of sailings from the Piscataqua River to Boston.

The captain of the *Watch and Wait*, guided his pinnace* up the Ipswich River the night before the sailing and took on the waiting passengers — Anthony Thacher, a Nonconformist churchman only four months from England, with his four children and a second wife, Elizabeth Jones Thacher, whom he had married six weeks before leaving London.

Elizabeth Thacher wore some of her wedding finery, a cloak of embroidered scarlet wool, to protect herself from the bone-chilling mists. The cloak may well have been fashioned by her husband, for on the passenger list, when Anthony Thacher sailed from London on the *James*, he was listed both as a curate in his brother's parish and as a tailor. (His father had been a tailor before him.) There is some evidence, however, that he may not have been a tailor and that this listing was only a subtle way of diverting officials from tracking down the dissenter. In any case,

---

* Fishing vessels of the day were usually called pinnaces until a Captain Robinson of Gloucester gave them the name of schooner — a new name for a two-masted vessel.

Elizabeth Thacher's fine scarlet coat was destined to see exceptional service for generations to come.

In addition to the Thacher family of seven, which included a cousin, were the Reverend John Avery* (who was also a cousin) and his wife and six children; three others believed to be either cousins or servants to help with the ten children; William H. Elliot, a passenger; and the four crew members — a total of twenty-three persons on board. This boat, until recently owned by Isaac Allerton of Marblehead, had been turned over, only two months earlier, to his son-in-law, Moses Maverick. The vessel was crowded and uncomfortable that night as it tossed about in recurrent squalls, but the captain wished to have everyone on board for sailing early the next morning. All were unprepared for what lay ahead.

Any storm whirls wild seas around Cape Ann, and this week-long storm, when the tide rose twenty feet, was to become the wildest storm in the memory of anyone in that part of New England. Not even Cape Ann Indians rememberd a more devastating storm.*

By afternoon the captain had the pinnace out in the bay, but the seas were already increasing. He tried tacking many times but made no headway against the powerful winds. On Friday, two days later, he gave up and tried to put in to the comparative safety of Sandy Bay Harbor to escape from the storm, which by then had picked up again to a force so terrifying that the group on the *Watch and Wait* could only huddle together in prayer.

The change of course came too late. The fury of the storm had already begun its destruction of the *Watch and Wait*. The patched sails split; the anchor dragged, then had to be cut loose; and the pinnace tossed unchecked as it plunged helplessly toward submerged rocks and certain doom. Anthony Thacher miraculously escaped with his wife and his own life, and he tells his own sad and moving story in the now famous letter that he wrote some weeks later to his brother in London.

*I must turn my drowned pen and shaking hand to indite the story of such sad news as never before this happened in New England. There was a league of perpetual friendship between my cousin Avery and myself never*

---

\* Both Anthony Thacher and John Avery had been highly regarded for their education and leadership.

\* This storm brought three now well known Cape Ann families — Andrews, Cogswells, and Burnhams — to Ipswich Harbor. En route from England to Pemaquid, they were driven by the gale into Ipswich, where they made their home. The same storm — of hurricane proportions — swept away William Tucker's house on the Isle of Shoals just to the north of Cape Ann, and the wreckage of the house was later found at Cape Cod.

to forsake each other to the death but to be partakers of each other's misery or welfare, as also of habitation in the same place. Now upon our arrival in New England there was an offer made to us. My cousin Avery was invited to Marblehead to be their pastor in due time, there being no church planted there as yet, but a town appointed to set up the trade of fishing, because many there (the most being fishermen) were something remiss in their behavior. My cousin Avery was unwilling to go there; and so refusing, we went to Newbury intending there to sit down.

But being solicited so often both by the men of the place and by magistrates and by Mr. Cotton and by most of the ministers, who alleged what a benefit we might be to the people there and also to the country and the Commonwealth, at length we embraced it and there consented to go. They of Marblehead forthwith sent a pinnace for us and our goods. We embarked at Ipswich August 11, 1635, with our families and substance bound for Marblehead we being in all twenty-three souls, namely: eleven in my cousin's family, seven in mine, and one Mr. William Elliot, sometimes of New Sarum, and four mariners. The next morning, having commended ourselves to God, with cheerful hearts we hoisted sail.

But the Lord suddenly turned our cheerfulness into mourning and lamentations for on the 14th day of August, 1635, about ten at night, having a fresh gale of wind, our sails being old and done were split. The mariners, because that it was night, would not put to new sails but resolved to cast anchor till the morning. But before light it pleased the Lord to send so mighty a storm as the like was never known in New England since the English came, nor in the memory of the Indians.

It was so furious that our anchors came home. Whereupon the mariners let out more cable which at last slipped away. Then our sailors knew not what to do, but we were driven before the wind and waves.

My cousin and I perceived our danger and solemnly recommended ourselves to God the Lord both of earth and seas, expecting with every wave to be swallowed up and drenched in the deep. And as my cousin, his wife, and my tender babes sat comforting and cheering each other in the Lord against ghastly death which every moment stared us in the face and sat triumphing in each other's forehead, we were by the violence and fury of the winds, by the Lord's permission, lifted upon a rock between two high rocks, yet all was one rock. But it raged with the stroke which came into the pinnace so as we were presently up to our middles as we sat.

The waves came furiously and violently over us and against us, but for reason of the rock's proportion could not lift us off but beat her all to pieces. Now look with me upon our distress and consider my misery who beheld the ship broken, the water in her and violently overwhelming as, my goods, and provisions swimming in the seas, my friends almost drowned, and mine own poor children so untimely (if I may term it without offense) before mine eyes drown and ready to be swallowed up and dashed to pieces against the rocks by the merciless waves, and myself ready to accompany them. In the same room whereat we sat, the master of the pinnace, not knowing what to do, our foremast was cut down, our mainmast broken in three pieces, the forepart of the pinnace beat away, our goods swimming about the seas, my children bewailing me, as not pitying themselves, and myself bemoaning them, poor souls, whom I had occasioned to such an end in their tender years, when as they would scarce be sensible to death, and so likewise my cousin, his wife and children; and both of us bewailing each other in our Lord and only Savior, Jesus Christ, in whom only we had comfort and cheerfulness, insomuch that from the greatest to the least of us there was not one screech or outcry made, but all as silent as sheep were contentedly resolved to die together lovingly, as since our acquaintance we had lived together friendly.

Now I was sitting in the cabin room door with my body in the room, when lo! one of the sailors by a wave being washed out of the pinnace was gotten again and coming into the cabin room over my back, cried out, "We are cast away! The Lord have mercy upon us! I have been washed over-board into the sea and am gotten in again." His screeches made me look forth; and looking toward the sea and seeing how we were, I turned myself to my cousin and the rest and spake these words: "O Cousin, it hath pleased God to cast us here between two rocks, the shore not far from us for I saw the tops of trees when I looked forth!"

Whereupon the master of the pinnace looking up at the scuttle hole of the quarterdeck, went out at it; but I never saw him afterwards. Then he that had been in the sea went out again by me and leaped over-board toward the rocks, whom afterwards also I could not see. Now none were left in the barque, that I knew or saw, but my cousin, his wife and his children, myself and mine and his maid servant. But my cousin thought I would have fled from him, and said unto me: "O Cousin, leave us not, let us die together," and reached forth his hand unto me.

Then I, letting go my son Peter's hand, took him by the hand said, "Cousin, I purpose not. Whither shall I go? I am willing to die with you and my poor children. God be merciful unto us, and receive us unto himself," adding these words, "The Lord is able to help and deliver."

He replied, saying, "Truth, Cousin, but what pleasure is we know not. I fear we have been too unthankful for former deliverances, but he hath promised to deliver us from sin and condemnation and to bring us safe to Heaven for all the sufficient satisfaction of Jesus Christ. This therefore we may challenge of him."

To which I replying said: "That is all the deliverance I desire and expect," which words I had no sooner spoken but by a mighty wave I was with the piece of barque washed out upon part of the rock, where the waves left me almost drowned. But recovering my feet I saw above me on the rock my daughter Mary, to whom I had no sooner gotten but my cousin Avery and his eldest son came to us, being all four of us washed out by one and the same wave. We went all into a small hole on the top of the rock, whence we called to those in the pinnace to come unto us, supposing we had been in more safety than they were in. My wife, seeing us there, crept up into the scuttle of the quarter-deck to come to us. But presently came another wave and dashing the pinnace all to pieces carried my wife away in the scuttle as she was, with the greater part of the quarter-deck unto the shore, where she was cast safely but her legs were something bruised, and much timber of the vessel was there also cast. She was sometime before she could get away being washed by the waves. All the rest that were in the barque were drowned in the merciless sea. We four by that wave were clean swept away from off the rock, also into the sea, the Lord in one instant of time disposing of fifteen souls of us according to His good pleasure and will. This pleasure and wonderful mercy to me was thus: standing on the rock as before you heard, with my eldest daughter, my cousin and his eldest son, looking upon and talking to them in the barque, whereas we were by that merciless wave washed off the rock as before you heard, God in His mercy caused me to fall by the stroke of the waves flat on my face, for my face was towards the sea. Insomuch that I was sliding off the rock into the sea, the Lord directed my toes into a joint in the rock's side as also the tops of some of my fingers with my right hand, by the means whereof, the wave leaving me, I remained so hanging on the rock only my head above the water, when on the left hand I espied a board or plank of the pinnace, and as I was reaching out my left hand to lay hold on it, by another wave coming over the top of the rock I washed away from the rock and by the violence of the wave was driven hither and thither in the sea a great while, and had many dashes against the rocks. At length, past hope of life and wearied in body and spirit I even gave over to nature and being ready to receive in the waters of death, I lifted up my heart and hands to God of Heaven (for note I had my senses remaining perfect with me all the time that I was under and in the water) who at that instant lifted my head above the top of the *water, that so I might breathe without any hindrance by the waters.*

*I stood bolt upright as if I had stood upon my feet but I felt no bottom nor had any footing to stand upon the waters. While I was thus above the waters I saw by me a piece of the mast as I suppose about three feet long, which I labored to catch in my arms, but suddenly I was overwhelmed with water and driven to and fro again, and at last I felt the ground with my right foot, when immediately whilst I was groveling on my face I presently recovering my feet was in the water up to my breast and through God's great mercy had my face unto the shore and not the sea. I made haste to get out, but was thrown down on my hands with the waves and so with safety crept to the dry shore, where blessing God, I turned to look about for my children and friends and saw neither nor any part of the pinnace, where I left them as I supposed, but I saw my wife about a butt\* length (\*a board log) from me, getting herself forth from amongst the timbers of the broken barque; but before I could get unto her she was gotten to shore. I was in the water after I was washed from the rock, before I came to the shore, a quarter of an hour at least.*

*When we were come to each other we went and sat under the bank, but fear of the sea roaring and our coldness would not suffer us there to remain. But we went up into the land and sat us down under a cedar tree which the wind had thrown down, where we sat about an hour, almost dead with cold. But now the storm was broken and the wind was calm. But the sea remained rough and fearful to us.*

*My legs were much bruised and so was my head, other hurts I had none, neither had I taken in much quantity of water, but my heart would not let me sit still any longer but I would go to see if any more were gotten to the land in safety, especially hoping to have met some of my poor children, but I could find none, either dead nor yet living. You condole with me my miseries, who now begun to consider my losses.*

*Now came to my remembrance the time and manner, how and when, I last saw and left my children and friends. One was severed from me sitting on the rock at my feet, the other three in the pinnace, my little babe (Ah, poor Peter) sitting in his sister Edith's arms, who, to the uttermost of her power sheltered him from the waters, my poor William standing close unto them, all three of them looking ruefully on me on the rock, their very countenances calling unto me to help them, whom I could neither go unto neither could they come to me, neither would the merciless waves afford me space or time to use any means at all either to help them or myself. Oh I yet see their cheeks, poor silent lambs pleading pity and help at my hands. Then on the other side to consider the loss of my friends, with the spoiling and loss of all our goods and provisions, myself cast upon an unknown land, in a wilderness, I know not where, nor how to get thence. Then it came to my mind how I had occasioned the death of my children, who caused them to leave their native land, who might have left them there, yea and might have sent some of them back again and cost me nothing. Those and such like thoughts do press upon my heavy heart very much. But I must let this pass, and will proceed on in the relation of God's goodness unto me in that desolate island on which I was cast. I and my wife were almost naked, both of us, and wet and cold even unto death. I found a knapsack cast upon the shore, in which I had a steel and flint and powder horn; going further I found a drowned goat; then I found a hat and my son William's coat, both of which I put on. I found also two cheeses and some butter driven ashore. Thus the Lord sent us some clothes to put on and food to sustain our new lives which we had lately given unto us, and means also to make a fire, for in a horn I had some gunpowder which, to my own and since to other men's admiration, was dry. So taking a piece of my wife's sackcloth which I dried in the sun, I struck fire and so dried and warmed our wet bodies; and then skinned the goat and having found a small brass pot we boiled some of her. Our drink was brackish water. Bread we had none. There we remained till Monday following; when about three of the clock in the afternoon, in a boat that came that way, we went off that desolate island, which I named after my name — Thacher's Woe — and the rock Avery his fall, to the end that their fall and loss and mine own might be in perpetual remembrance. In the isle lieth buried the body of my cousin's eldest daughter, whom I found dead on the shore. On Tuesday following, in the afternoon, we arrived at Marblehead.*

## A New Life for Anthony Thacher

Word of the tragedy spread quickly throughout all the New England settlements, and many benefactors, including the scattered few in Marblehead, came to the rescue of the bereaved and destitute couple. It was then that the Massachusetts General Court, sitting at Salem, voted to grant Anthony 40 marks in English money (said to be about $88.88) "out of the treasury toward his late greate losses."

In March of the following year the Court, still in a merciful frame of mind, agreed "to grant to Mr. Anthony Thacher the small island at the head of Cape Ann upon which hee was preserved from shipwreck as his inheritance."

Cape Ann would have been the richer if Anthony Thacher had claimed "his inheritance," but he and Elizabeth chose to remain at Marblehead where their rescuers had taken them. He was then forty-seven years of age and, understandably, could have given way to despair. Yet, even in the face of such loss, he assumed the church work that John Avery had been called to do, and in doing this he gained new courage.

Within a few months Anthony had settled John Avery's modest estate, having been named by the courts as administrator. The estate included a few debts owed to Avery (all but one collected), a sow and some pigs, and ten bushels of Indian corn. Within three years, not only had Anthony recovered sufficiently from his personal tragedy to begin rearing a new family; he had also traveled across the bay to Plymouth. Here he renewed acquaintance with old friends among the *Mayflower* Pilgrims whom he had met years before at the Dutch town of Leyden, prior to the *Mayflower* sailing. In those early days, at age twenty-one, he had assisted his brother, Peter, who was rector of a church at Salisbury. The men and women of their congregation held similar Puritan beliefs, and some years later he had followed them to America, taking with him Peter's fifteen-year-old-son, Thomas. (On the day of the *Watch and Wait* shipwreck Thomas had become apprehensive about the storm and changed his mind about sailing on the ship.)

Some of the *Mayflower* Pilgrims had already explored Cape Cod areas for possible expansion of their farms and settlements, and early in 1639 Anthony Thacher joined his friends there. Elizabeth, who was pregnant, did not immediately follow, and on March 7 a son, John, was born at Marblehead.

Later that year Elizabeth and John joined Anthony, who by then had built a house on his own land. The colonial court had appointed Anthony and two other men grantees of the land that was later to be Yarmouth, Massachusetts.

Anthony was the first man listed there as a freeman. This man, so recently bereft of all he owned, now took possession of 130 acres of upland and 26 acres of meadowland, in addition to Thachers Island at Cape Ann.

If Anthony Thacher had remained at Cape Ann, in all probability he would have lived much the same kind of life. In these early days, Cape Cod settlers lived in fear of wolves as they did at Cape Ann; disputes arose over land use and were settled by Myles Standish, as also at Cape Ann; and he went on with his life near the sea — farming; fishing; raising cattle; and, according to reports, he "planted pears for his heirs." Meanwhile, he and Elizabeth added to their family another son, Judah, and a daughter, Bethia. Descendants say that for generations of Thachers each child was

Thacher cradle, hand carved by Anthony Thacher or his son John, when on exhibition at the Heritage Museum in Lexington, Mass.

christened in the tattered scarlet cloak so carefully preserved by Elizabeth Thacher.

Although by this time Anthony had ceased to be an active part of the Cape Ann story, his name, linked forever to his island, became such an important factor in Cape Ann history that it seems worthwhile to recognize his character and strength of purpose. Believing that he had been treated with great compassion in his time of need, he devoted the rest of his life to helping others. Though he was involved in controversies with Indians several times, there is no evidence to indicate that he was anything but a man of peace, even to the extent of giving up many acres of his own land to settle differences. He lived a life of simplicity, and he pursued an amazingly long list of duties while serving others.

Almost immediately he became a member of the Council of War, was appointed town treasurer and town clerk, and was given many of the powers of a court of justice. In addition, he was licensed to join couples in marriage; to execute wills; to "observe newcomers who were there without permission"; to observe those who failed to attend church; to en-courage education; to provide for the poor; to inspect lead, powder, shot, and liquor; as well as to draw wine. One of his duties, perhaps to him one of the most important because he knew at first hand of its value to mariners, was to inspect anchors. Toward the end of his life the courts and a new law provided for selectmen, and he was appointed along with four other men to fill this new post. He served two years until his death in 1667 at age seventy-eight, after which he was honored for his wisdom and his piety. His heirs claim that he was buried under one of the pear trees that he had planted so long before. Whether this is true or not, an ancient pear tree still stands in Anthony Thacher's meadow near the sea.

## A New Life for the Island

Along with the pear tree and the Yarmouth acres, Thachers Island at Cape Ann remained in the Thacher family for 80 years. It was apparently considered a valuable holding, for in the next 200 years it changed hands only six times. At this time a Thacher heir, Col. John Appleton of Ipswich, sold to a Gloucester settler, the Reverend John White, "thirty acres, more or less, a certain island lying and being off ye town of Gloucester, for 100 pounds."

John White owned the island for ten years to use as pasturage for his oxen, a yoke of oxen then considered to be equal in value to a house and barn. He eventually sold it to another Gloucester man, Joseph Allen, making on the deal a profit of seventy five pounds "in public bills." The deed described the island as "commonly called Thacher's Island, containing 5 and 20 acres, more or less."

The family of Joseph Allen then pastured oxen there, as many as fourteen at a time, until 1771, when Allen heirs sold the island to three Gloucester men — John Low, Samuel Plummer, and William Ellery — who in turn sold it to a committee of six men* who had been authorized by the Massachusetts Bay Colony to buy the island and "erect a light house or houses, and a convenient house for the keeper."

The importance of establishing lights on Thachers was now publicly recognized for the first time. Probably with the Thacher shipwreck in mind, as well as dozens of other ship losses, some Marblehead merchants and mariners made this first move toward erecting the lighthouses on Thachers, and in the petition, presented to the General Court by John Hancock (who held large shipping interests), they proposed to tax Boston shipowners for "light money" to cover the costs of building and maintaining the lighthouses and the lights.

* John Hancock, Capt. Nathaniel Allen, Maj. Richard Reed, Capt. Richard Derby, John Erving, and Capt. John Patrick Tracy.

Such an assessment was almost as unpopular as the British tax on tea, and many merchants refused to pay it, making it difficult to collect the necessary funds. As the towers went up so did the costs, and there was no easy way to pay the bills for construction.

Nevertheless, the plan was official, and though important decisions still had to be made, the work of constructing the two lighthouses on Thachers, and a dwelling house for the keeper, began immediately.

# 1771–1784

*I*N 1771 there were already ten lighthouses operating in the thirteen American colonies, and the light station at Cape Ann was to be the eleventh – and last – lighthouse to be built under British rule. The Thachers Island lights, therefore, were among the foundation stones for the nation's lighthouse system that functioned until 1939 when the Coast Guard took over.

Since Thachers was located on the direct commercial route from Europe and Canada to Boston, the decision to place lights there, as necessary aids to navigation,* was a welcome one. The lights would also serve to warn mariners of the dreaded Londoner (earlier called Gannet Rock and earlier still, Fisher Rock), a partly submerged reef located a half-mile south-southeast of the island.

The Londoner lies mostly underwater at high tide, 90 feet long and 57 feet wide at its widest point, and it was here that a schooner from London once foundered, thereby giving the rock its present name, the Londoner. The close relationship of the Londoner to Thachers became apparent when measurements from this rock determined the site locations of the north and south towers.

Up until this time little thought had been given to actual site locations of any lighthouses, although politicians considered it evidence of strong political backing to have a lighthouse built in their constituency. Politics crept into nearly all decisions involving lighthouses, but it was lighthouse

---

* The first aids to navigation for Cape Ann were the bonfires built on the shore by women and children as beacons to guide their fishermen safely home.

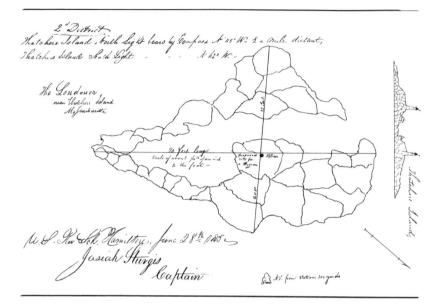

Sketch of the Londoner made from the U.S. Revenue Schooner *Hamilton* on June 28, 1845.

engineers, rather than politicians, who made the final decision to build the last of the colonial lighthouses as twins. At that early date engineers believed that certain characteristics, easily recognized by mariners, must distinguish one light from another.*

After this decision had been made, and the actual sites for the twin towers chosen, north and south, there was still scarcely a level place on which to build them. Boulders tossed up by ages of Atlantic storms had to be cleared away before construction could begin.

No records can be found of the men who built the first twin towers by hand labor and oxen, but the work of clearing, selecting, and moving the rocks went on without delay. The end of 1771 saw the completion of the two 45-foot towers.

## Lights On

On December 2, 1771, Forefathers' Day (a holiday then observed in honor of the Pilgrims), lights of the twin lighthouses at Thachers flickered

---

* Later on, the Coast Guard considered that the more modern revolving lens provided the necessary distinctions; later still, the service computed the number of flashes.

their candle flame over Sandy Bay for the first time. The lights could be seen, though dimly, from any point on the southern and eastern coasts of Cape Ann. On the mainland, Cape Anners, nearly all mariners, peered out at the new lights with the greatest satisfaction and at once dubbed them with affection, "Ann's Eyes."

At last, after an interval of 135 years, the island of rock and reef that had saved the life of Anthony Thacher and his wife, Elizabeth, had begun its historic vigil of ceaselessly beaming its warning across the open sea. Thereafter, Ann's Eyes were to become an eternal memorial to the Thacher family and to the tragedy of the *Watch and Wait*.

The memorial, so distinctive, so high in purpose, was nevertheless destined to struggle endlessly for its very existence. Beset by one obstacle after another, from the moment the lights first flickered on, the island's trials and heartbreaks loomed almost as constant as the storms that lashed it.

Yet, in spite of the many stumbling blocks, the great work of keeping the lights burning to save one more ship and even to save one more life — so important to so many — was to continue for centuries, with each family living there furthering these goals in its own way. To keep Ann's Eyes aglow became a never-ending labor of love.

Although the actual work of building the twin towers was completed in 1771, it was 1773 before the Massachusetts Bay Colony officially established the Cape Ann Light Station. This must have been a great day of celebration for all of Cape Ann, as well as for sailors and shippers along the coast to Boston, yet scarcely had the work of the new lighthouses — that of saving lives and ships — got under way when it became apparent that the choice of a light keeper would produce the first of many setbacks for the Cape Ann Light Station.

## First Lighthouse Keeper

The first lighthouse keeper, Capt. James Kirkwood, was appointed by the colonial court to tend the lights, to keep them burning around the clock, and to care for the sheep and cattle pastured there for his food.

Captain Kirkwood had been hired for a period of two and a half years at a salary of "100 pounds, six shillings, and firewood," for himself and two assistants. This amounted to about $300 per year. It was still difficult, however, to collect the "light money," even though construction of the lighthouses was all but completed, and Kirkwood complained that for eighteen months he had received no pay except in the form of provisions.

Since neither of Kirkwood's assistants had received the four and five dollars, respectively, due them per month, Kirkwood wrote to the provincial court a stirring plea for his back pay:

*Since December, 1771, I have attended this duty, though a very hard one, with no allowances except for provisions. Neither of my assistants has been paid.*

*The island being at some distance from the mainland and much exposed to hard gales of wind and extreme cold in the winter which together with the lighthouses and dwelling not being quite finished make it a very uncomfortable habitation, and attended with great difficulty, as the lighthouses stand at a great distance from one another (tho very properly placed for the safety and benefit of trade). The ruffness of the way makes it very difficult and dangerous passing and repassing from one lighthouse to another, especially at nights, in the winter season, being obliged to do it at ten at night and two in the morning to the endangering of their lives and limbs.*

*It is a full mile from the island to the mainland and sometimes for three or four weeks they have not dared to venture ashore because of the boisterousness of the sea, so that at such times (though they should be in the utmost distress) they can't get any assistance or supplies from the shore.*

Kirkwood went on to point out that there was "too much to do when all were well and if one of them were laid up the duty was very fatiguing for the rest."

As a result of Kirkwood's pleas for pay, he was reimbursed eleven pounds for the eighteen months, but all this led to his dismissal as "unpatriotic."

Feeling between Torys and Patriots was now running high on Cape Ann, and Kirkwood was accused of being a Tory. "Why else," his hecklers asked, "would a man work for eighteen months without pay?"

In spite of the accusations against Kirkwood, on June 24, 1775, the provincial congress approved and signed an order to pay him sixty pounds for an additional year's salary as keeper of the lights on Thachers Island. In addition to his salary he was to receive eighteen pounds, thirteen shillings as reimbursement for maintaining the buildings and "for other work done there" — clearing the rocks. One of his "fringe benefits" was to be a form of early health insurance — "Pay for a box of medicine, and other necessities as per his account."

If the government trusted Captain Kirkwood with an expense account, however, it was clear that many Cape Anners living on the mainland trusted his politics not at all. As the Revolution intensified, Cape Ann fishermen, scouting the island, watched Kirkwood with suspicion and now condemned him as being unpatriotic. Word spread of possible traitorous activities, and eventually rumors reached the newly formed militia at Gloucester. Then one day, under orders, the militia took to boats and sailed to the island, with scarcely the creak of a sail to announce their coming. Kirkwood had no way to escape from his adversaries, and they dislodged him forthwith, never waiting to prove his innocence or guilt.

The last word of Kirkwood was that he escaped to Canada, leaving behind all his possessions. Although Kirkwood's belongings on the island were probably few, he must have lamented the loss of a chest of drawers he had made on the island for his British bride. Whether his bride ever reached Cape Ann, or whether James Kirkwood ever returned to her by way of Canada after the Revolution, remains a well-kept secret of the island.

The chest, however, disappeared from the island only to reappear some 150 years later, when it was sold for a modest sum. Now owned by Helen Porter of Gloucester, the chest is a treasure of early craftsmanship, complete with its fittings of burnished British brass.

The service of Thachers first lightkeeper had come to an inglorious end, but the day Kirkwood so unceremoniously left the island was even more disastrous for the new lighthouses and for all seagoing vessels. Kirkwood's dismissal extinguished the lights on Thachers Island. For the first time since they were installed, the twins no longer beamed their warning through the fog and darkness.

Order issued by the Provincial Congress to pay James Kirkwood his back salary.

Fishermen and coasting vessels felt the loss at once, but it was not until after peace was restored, and the United States government took over from the British, that a new lighthouse keeper eventually filled the oil pans and lighted the wicks in the twin sentinels of Thachers.

### Fishermen Remain Vigilant

All this time, however, Cape Anners remained watchful of activity about their shores and the island. While local fishermen feared that the lights would never come on again, they took upon themselves the responsibility of aiding vessels in distress.

Not long after Kirkwood's removal, in November of that same year (1775), alert Cape Ann fishermen sighted a suspicious-looking vessel lying offshore between Straitsmouth Island and Thachers. The observant fishermen at once recognized this to be a British ship, probably carrying supplies for troops at Boston.

Twenty fishermen hastily gathered arms and commandeered one of their own fishing boats, the schooner *Lee*, in Sandy Bay Harbor. Then, under a veil of fog, they put to sea as silently as their predecessors in the militia and captured the alien vessel without resistance, taking crew and cargo into Sandy Bay Harbor.

The cargo was a deckload of cattle, a hold full of ammunition, and (as reported by historian Ebenezer Pool) "A wonderful great brass mortar," said to be "the noblest piece of ordnance ever landed in America." This prize the captors immediately christened "The Congress"!

When word of the capture of the *Nancy* reached General Washington, then at Cambridge, he sent back the message that Cape Ann fishermen were to keep the vessel for themselves, along with the oxen and beef, as their share of the prize. He asked only that they send him the naval stores and the additional provisions they had found on the vessel. This division of the spoils was entirely agreeable to the fishermen, although they had work ahead — the oxen had to be hoisted overboard by their horns and then towed ashore!

There was more to the story of the *Nancy*. This British ship became by chance an interesting sidelight to the Thachers Island story. During the capture, under the fog screen, one British seaman managed to escape from the *Nancy*. He swam four miles before touching shore, bruised and exhausted, but he lived to launch the first romance to be connected with the island. As he lay nearly unconscious on the wet sand, young Mary Andrews of Pigeon Cove found him, revived him, and helped him walk through the woods to her home on Andrews' Point. Here she nursed him back to health. She asked few questions of his British past, and the two were married within six months.

### The Island Is Abandoned

Unfortunately, neither romantic love affairs nor the excitement of battle offshore had any effect on the relighting of the Thachers Island candles. The island had had no lightkeeper for almost five years, but in 1780 an even worse calamity struck the island. Not only were the lights out, but the towers, the keeper's house, and all the equipment (still only nine years old) were ordered abandoned! Little hope remained that the lights would ever again shine from Thachers.

Ships foundered on all sides of Thachers as no lights warned them of the Londoner. The island was now deserted, and the memorial to the Thacher family was almost certainly doomed to be forgotten before it could get fully under way. No longer was there a Cape Ann Light Station that had begun with so much promise in 1773.

In a very short time the property that had offered reassurance to vessels in distress began to deteriorate, and as it decayed vandals aggravated the situation by removing the government property.

Somewhat belatedly, an aroused government appointed a committee of one, Stephen Choate, to take charge of the property; his orders were to lease it each year "for as much as it will fetch." Evidently, government officials felt that it might be possible to rent out lighthouse duties to anyone who would be willing to gamble on collecting his "light money." No one fell for the plan, and Stephen Choate proceeded to sell off everything that could be moved from the island, returning the money to the U. S. Treasury.

Although the hope of "renting out" the lighthouse property failed, the General Court did not give up. It appointed Gloucester businessman Peter Coffin to repair and put in order the Cape Ann lighthouses and to "demand and receive" all the articles that had been removed.

In 1784 the General Court paid both Coffin and Samuel Whittemore for putting the island houses in order. Some assurance that Thachers had at last returned to its original purpose of saving lives and ships came in February when a court order directed Coffin and Whittemore to sell to Thachers Island lighthouses (and to Boston lighthouses as well) twelve cords of wood and thirty pounds of candles. The wood and candles became the means of getting the north and south towers of Thachers back in business.

## A New Light Keeper Is Appointed

Samuel Huston* met the requirements of the General Court for a new lightkeeper. His appointment not only pleased the Court but also met with approval of the commissary general, who directed that "a small boat and a small barn" be built for the new lightkeeper.

No sooner had Sam Huston hauled up his new dory on Thachers, however, than he realized the place had gone to "wreck and ruin." Undaunted, Huston resolved to restore things at once, and his first move was to petition the court for supplies:

> *100 squares of glass*
> *100 pounds of putty*
> *2 tin flasks*
> *2 iron kettles*
> *60 bushels of charcoal*
> *12 cords of wood*
> *100 pounds of candles*
> *50 pounds of cotton and oil*
> *other supplies as should be needed*

The General Court granted the supplies to Huston and his two assistants, and in addition voted to pay them 120 pounds annually, as well as profits arising "from the improvement of the island."

Evidently, the Court anticipated that the eighty acres would be either tilled or used as pasturage, considering there was "quite an amount of arable tillage." Although Anthony Thacher's island was back in business, it now appeared that there was about as much interest in farming as in tending the lights!

---

* Huston married Sally Rowe and was the ancestor of Gloucester's D. O. Frost family.

# *1784-1814*

*T*HE SUPPLIES were on hand – oil, candles, and wood – but Sam Huston had to putty 100 panes of glass before the glow of the candles could once again reach a ship heading toward disaster on the rocks.

Meanwhile, in the months that followed the Declaration of Independence, the wheels of a new government had begun to turn. Fifteen years went by, however, before it was financially able to take over from the young states the maintenance of lighthouses so necessary for the saving of lives and ships along the Atlantic coastline.

Even as Sam Huston worked, he was called upon to assist the crew of the schooner *Abigail* from Salem, lost on the Londoner in a storm in April 1790.

## Colonial Lighthouses Ceded to United States

While Huston puttied all those panes of glass, on June 10, 1790, the Commonwealth of Massachusetts approved an act that officially ceded to the United States all the lighthouses along the Massachusetts coast, including "the two lighthouses situate on Thacher's Island, so called, in the County of Essex, together with the lands and tenements thereunto belonging, the property of this Commonwealth."

The Commonwealth stipulated further:

*provided nevertheless, that if the United States shall at any time hereafter neglect to keep lighted, and in repair, any one or more of the lighthouses aforesaid, that then the grant of such lighthouses so neglected shall be void and of no effect.... And provided further that if the United States should at any time take compensation for said property, it shall reimburse the Commonwealth in a like amount.*

Unfortunately, and in spite of supreme efforts by merchants and mariners to establish and maintain these eleven light stations, the lighthouse system was destined to suffer many years of weak management, political patronage, and waste. Confusion reigned, and from the beginning Thachers suffered along with the other light stations.

While in the colonial period each of the thirteen colonies generally looked after its own needs, the new system of lighthouses was first placed under the management of the Treasury Department. As time went on, it was shuffled back and forth from Treasury to Commerce and back again briefly to Treasury. All these moves reflected mismanagement and increasing chaos until, eventually, the entire system was relegated to the fifth auditor in the Department of the Treasury, who now received it as part of his bookkeeping chores. To add to the problem, the fifth auditor, said to be "no more than a glorified bookkeeper," had no maritime background whatsoever, and to make matters even worse, he had no conception of his responsibility for the saving of lives — the primary reason for the existence of the lighthouses in the first place.

The man with these shortcomings was a political appointee, and for years little could be done about the situation. Obviously, the struggling lighthouse system needed more than mere bookkeeping.

Although there were, within a few years, other lighthouses along the Atlantic coast — nineteen in Massachusetts, eight more in Rhode Island and Connecticut, and eighteen along the coast from New York to Georgia — a total of forty-five — the twin lights at Thachers, from the very beginning, were considered to be among the most important. Ranking with the Hatteras, Eddystone, and Boston lights, they were the first to be seen when en route from England to Massachusetts Bay, and the last to be seen when leaving Boston for England, the eastern parts of Maine, and the Canadian provinces.

If Thachers was so important, why were the lights still unlighted? Obviously, the new nation was busy getting itself organized, but in 1792, after Huston had replaced all 100 panes of glass and otherwise reclaimed the island, he left the island and Joseph Sayward replaced him.

Now, along with the fledgling government struggling to make ends meet, lightkeeper Sayward began the struggle for his personal survival on Thachers. When he accepted his duties in 1793, his pay was set at the rate of $400 for principal keepers of the Thachers Island's lights, but President Washington soon changed this. In a letter dated July 18, 1793, Washington ordered that the pay be reduced to "266 and 2/3 dollars." This move was probably made for two reasons. Not only was the Treasury Department having a hard time making ends meet, but officials with little knowledge of lightkeepers or their work considered accommodations at Thachers most "favorable." With cattle to raise and their own vegetable gardens to harvest, officials contended, "the keepers can live on less."

So it was that Joseph Sayward, under these conditions, relighted the twins at Thachers Island.

Cape Anners rejoiced to have Ann's Eyes shining anew from Thachers, though the weak whale-oil lamps no longer satisfied commercial interests. For now, welcome as they were, the lights were so disappointingly dim that they were barely visible from the mainland.

Experiments to improve the lights were going on all the time, up and down the coast. Yet most lighthouses from 1750 to 1800 still used a lamp with flat wicks and whale oil, which quickly smoked up the glass and dimmed the lights. Cleaning the glass required many hours of Sayward's time, and it was partly because of the unsatisfactory lamps that more lives and ships were lost.

In 1795, less than three years after Sayward moved to the island, two ships and their crews were lost off Cape Ann. These were the *Margaret*, sailing from Amsterdam, and the American ship *Industry*, sailing from Portsmouth to Boston.

Meanwhile, a Swiss scientist, Aimé Argand, developed a lamp with a hollow wick, a lamp that would eventually reach the Cape Ann Light Station. This lamp was an acknowledged improvement over the old wicks still in use at Thachers and other light stations, as not only was it almost smoke-free, but it burned with the incredible brilliance of seven candles!

British lighthouses began to use this new lamp right away, with a reflector added for even brighter light, but for a time the United States continued its experiments to improve the quality of both the light and the fuel of its lamps. The United States had been somewhat clumsy as it moved through a variety of fuels from candles to fish oil, olive oil, porpoise oil, lard, and whale oil. These efforts resulted in the so-called Spider lamp, a simple device of four wicks in a pan of whale oil.

At first this new lamp appeared to be superior to the old flat-wick type of lamp, but in the long run the Spider lamps brought little satisfaction, for they tended to give off fumes that burned the eyes and nostrils of the lightkeepers. In addition, these lights required that as many as twelve or

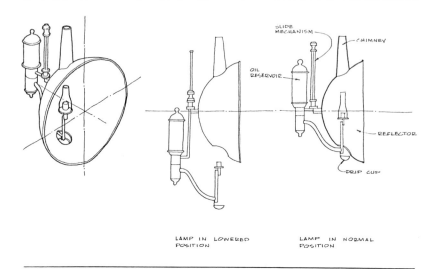

SLIDE MECHANISM

CHIMNEY

OIL RESERVOIR

REFLECTOR

DRIP CUP

LAMP IN LOWERED POSITION

LAMP IN NORMAL POSITION

Drawing of the Argand lamp by David Battle.

more pans be kept full of fuel oil, while the keepers had to make sure that all wicks were lighted and that all panes of glass were kept free of smoke.

The Spider lamp, while never entirely satisfactory, nevertheless remained in use in some lighthouses until 1812 — and at Thachers even longer.

### Aimé Argand's Lamp Used in American Lighthouses

Word of Argand's lamp eventually reached lighthouse officials in America, and it was an unemployed Boston ship captain, Winslow Lewis, who had watched the lights develop, who brought it to their attention. Lewis was an inventor of sorts himself, as well as a mariner, and a shrewd businessman, as it turned out, who persuaded the United States government to adopt the lamp of the Swiss inventor, Argand, to be used in place of the Spider lamps.

By 1810 Lewis had devised a reflector of his own to be attached to the Argand lamp; through his friends in Congress he then arranged to demonstrate the superiority of this light. The demonstration was held in Boston, and it aroused such enthusiasm for the Argand lamp that Lewis immediately set about to obtain a patent for Argand's lamp but with Lewis's own reflector added, and then he offered to sell it to the United States government.

To do this, Lewis arranged a second demonstration, this one to take place in the south tower at Thachers Island off Cape Ann. He proceeded to invite Henry Dearborn, then the collector of customs at Boston, who, after this official test at Thachers, urged Secretary of the Treasury Albert Gallatin to accept Lewis's offer. In his package deal, Lewis proposed fitting out forty-nine lighthouses — all the country owned at the time — for the sum of $26,950.

The deal was to include an additional $33,050 to pay Lewis for his patent, making a total of $60,000, for which Lewis agreed to maintain the lights for a period of seven years. The patent, according to Lewis's critics, was no more than Argand's lamp with the slight difference in the reflector, but government officials overlooked this fact and Lewis, with great satisfaction, began to install the lights. Unfortunately, the War of 1812 came along and interrupted the project, with but forty of the forty-nine lamps installed, and it was 1815 before the last nine lamps were in place, completing the contract with Lewis.

While the Treasury Department apparently accepted the Argand lamp without reservations, keepers reported problems with them almost immediately. First, they said, "The lenses have a greenish tinge that reduces the power of the lights instead of increasing them."

Even with some improvements noted, the lights still fell short of the power of those along the British and Scottish coasts. Lightkeepers traced the trouble to the "parabolic" reflector — a curved cone design — which Lewis had made of so thin a metal that it soon lost its shape and thus its use. Critics referred to it with scorn as a "barber's basin," and inspectors protested at the reflector's inadequacy.

"It becomes a sphere instead of a parabola," they said. Yet this failure was not the whole problem. The reflectors were "silvered," and routine cleaning tended to wear off the silver.

In spite of the shortcomings of the new light, most accepted it as an improvement over the old Spider lamps, but the very acceptance of this Argand lamp for lighthouse service was an unfortunate step for the Thachers Island twins, as well as for most other lighthouses along the coast.

For one thing, it increased the duties of the lighthouse keepers more than ever, for reflectors had to be kept clean, and the new system required the keepers to care for twelve to fifteen lamps. This duty was made even more arduous, as shorter chimneys caused the reflectors to blacken quickly.

Despite the obvious shortcomings of Lewis's Argand lamp and parabolic reflector, no one denied that it was a great improvement over the old Spider lamp. Not only did it give off a brighter light — all of 7 candlepower —

but, to the satisfaction of the government, it used only half as much fuel and therefore it cost only half as much! Unfortunately, the government's adoption of the Argand lamp resulted in its overlooking a far better lighting device just being developed.

Officials completely disregarded the Fresnel lens, developed by a French physicist and inventor. They did so mostly in the interest of saving money, but also because of their own incompetence, thus causing the quality of the United States lighthouses to remain inferior to European lighthouses for at least forty years.

While all this experimenting with lights for the lighthouses was going on, Sayward was growing old in the lighthouse service on Thachers Island. He had served for over twenty years, from 1792 to 1814, and was considered to be "old and feeble." He found it harder and harder to climb the spiral staircases; to keep the oil containers filled; or, for that matter, even to tend his cattle.

Besides this, the War of 1812 brought renewed fears for the safety of the Cape Ann shoreline, and that same year the American merchantman *Alfred*, sailing from Russia to Boston, was lost in a January storm off Cape Ann. Although wartime aggressors recognized the constant need for lighthouses and usually left them alone, there were occasional forays, and one day in 1814 the enemy went ashore on Thachers. When they dug up some of Sayward's potatoes, the aging lighthouse keeper was helpless to defend his garden. As the war drew to a close, the job of lightkeeper was offered to his son, James, but the younger Sayward spurned the offer, saying, "The salary of $250 per year is insufficient," and the search began for a new lighthouse keeper for the twin lights of Thachers.

# 4

## 1814-1828

*A*ARON WHEELER, a fifty-four-year-old Pigeon Cove man, replaced Sayward, but the appointment immediately created new political dissension, and though Wheeler served another twenty years, the controversy was to haunt the island for thirty-five years.

In spite of the opposition to his appointment, Wheeler went about his work with goodwill. Not only did he tend the lights, but he also undertook the heavy work of rock clearing begun by James Kirkwood a generation earlier.

The reason for this enthusiasm for the extra work was soon apparent, for Wheeler was to benefit from it. There was talk of building a new and more comfortable dwelling house for the lighthouse keeper.

Discussions for building a better dwelling house for the keeper of the Cape Ann lights had gone on for a number of years. The project posed many problems, not the least of which was clearing the rough land by hand, and Wheeler set about helping the government by clearing the enormous boulders from the 300-yard space between the twin towers, and to "surface down" the rocks where the house was to sit.

Details of the new building were drawn up with care, and the articles of agreement were signed by Henry Dearborn, representing the United States government, and the contractor, a man of many talents, none other than Capt. Winslow Lewis. Lewis agreed to "build a stone dwelling house for the keeper of Thacher Island and the lighthouses thereon."

The original stone house as it appears today with additions.

### Construction of the Stone House

The house, when completed, was 34 feet long and 20 feet wide, with one story 8 feet high, divided into two rooms. The cellar under the house was "rock-stoned" with rocks from the island, and the walls were 6 feet high and 2 feet thick, "laid up with good lime mortar." The walls of the house were likewise 2 feet thick and "laid up with lime mortar and split stone."

A chimney went up in the center of the house, and in each room a fireplace was built, to include an oven on one side, with an iron or stone mantel, all lathed and plastered and protected with a double flooring.

Plans called for "a sufficient number of windows, well glazed, with shutters and proper fastenings." Perhaps with storms in mind, the doors were hung with iron hinges, thumb latches, and were equipped with "good locks." In addition, inside walls were lathed and plastered and "whitewashed twice over," — with all the woodwork, both inside and outside the house, receiving "two coats of good paint."

The structure included a porch in the rear of the house, "ten feet by twelve in the clear and as high as the eaves of the house." An entry contained stairs that went into one of the garret chambers, and a rectangular roof covered the house "with good shingles."

The house cost $1,415, and Lewis promised in writing to complete the work "by December 1 next in a faithful and workmanlike manner."

The new house was the first house to be built since the towers and early dwelling house forty-five years before, and it must have seemed quite sumptuous in comparison with that first structure, which was probably little more than a fisherman's shack for the lighthouse keeper.

Aaron Wheeler's appointment as keeper continued to meet with disapproval, and from time to time his adversaries redoubled their efforts to remove him. Yet, in spite of all the criticism, he stubbornly clung to his post. Besides his new house and his annual salary of £250, he received a bonus of $100 for his work of clearing the land. In addition to all this, he discovered another source of income—he and a friend from the mainland, Ebenezer Pool, went fishing!

Apparently the fishing was good in 1819, for the two men "freighted" from Thachers Island to Boston 1,000 quintals* of fish.

Although Wheeler's critics must have wondered how much time he spent wiping soot from the glass in the towers, there is little evidence to indicate that the lights were neglected, and they remained, as always, the most important work of the island. While the lights saved countless vessels, however, Atlantic storms still took their frightful toll. In this decade the sloop *Meteor* was lost on the Londoner, and on December 10, 1831, an unidentified vessel was lost a mere 100 yards off Thachers.

When devastating storms such as these wracked the island, it was often many days before Wheeler and Pool could return to their fishing, and while Wheeler went about his lighthouse duties, including extensive repairs, his friend, Ebenezer Pool, dreamed of pirate gold.

"With a mineral rod," Ebenezer said in later years, "I often dug on the island, looking for a pot!"

* One quintal = 100 pounds.

## 1828-1849

*D*REAMS OF GOLD and prof-
itable fishing, along with political
wrangling mingled for years with
the routine lightkeeping duties of the island. Meanwhile, with a sturdy
dwelling house completed and in use it was again time in 1828 — a mere
twelve years later — to make alterations on the by then fifty-seven-year-
old lighthouses.

To James Thayer and Noah Humphry of Hingham went the bid to
renew all the woodwork of the towers. Details of the proposed work were
itemized in longhand on the contract:

*Arches to be turned on top of the towers.*

*Soapstone decks laid with a scuttle on one side through which to enter
the lantern.*

*Scuttle door and ratchets to be covered with copper.*

*A new iron lantern to be installed in each tower.*

*Posts for lantern to be one inch and three quarters square and sunk
four feet deep into stonework.*

*Height and diameter of lantern sufficient to admit iron sash in each
octagon, and each octagon to contain twenty-one lights [panes] of twelve
by twelve glass.*

*Tables of the sashes to be three quarters of an inch thick.*

*Best quality glass, double thickness, from the New England Crown Glass
Manufactury, except*

*Lower tier filled with copper.*

*In one of the octagons to be a framed door covered with copper, 4 feet* by 2, to shut light into rabbets to be secured by a turn button.

Top of lantern to be a dome formed by 16 iron rafters concentrating in an iron hoop 9 inches wide.

Dome to be covered with copper, thirty ounces to the square foot, to be riveted to the hoop of the lantern.

On dome install a traversing ventilator, 17 inches high and 12 inches in diameter.

A vane to be secured in the above, 27 inches long and 12 inches wide.

Ventilator and vane to be framed with iron and covered with copper.

Iron railing round the lantern.

Posts for railing to be one inch and a quarter square connected by two railings three quarters of an inch square.

An electrical copper rod, three quarters of an inch in diameter, on each tower.

Towers to be whitewashed.

Lanterns and all woodwork, except stairs, to be painted twice over.

Doors to have strong hinges, latches, and locks.

Lanterns in each tower fitted with new lighting apparatus "in the same manner as other U.S. lighthouses."

In each tower 15 patent frames and 15 reflectors.

Lamps to be fitted with oil heaters, stove, and funnel; fitted to turn with the frame, each to have one spare lamp and one 14 gallon cannister and wick and tube box.

To include tin oil butts, to hold 600 gallons "like those in the lighthouses," frames for the butts to stand on, butts to be painted with three coats.

For the Thachers Island twins, of course, all this work must be in duplicate!

While the work went on, the problem of keeping the lights burning without interruption had to be solved. The contract called for entirely new lighting apparatus, with the lamps to be ready for lighting within six days after the old lamps were extinguished. In the meantime, a temporary light was to be kept lighted in each tower to equal four Argand lamps, the new lights to be installed in one tower before the old ones were extinguished in the other tower.

All the old materials were to go to the contractors, and the work was to be completed by June 1, 1828, at a cost of $2,300. By this time, however, Aaron Wheeler, too, was growing old in the lighthouse service, but it was not until January 1834 that a relative (probably a distant cousin) finally replaced him.

## Troubled Waters for the Wheelers

The younger man, Austin Wheeler, stayed for a brief three years, perhaps cutting his service short because he had only one hand to do the work of two, and in turn he was replaced by his brother, Charles.

So it happened that the Wheelers — Aaron, Austin, and Charles (all of Pigeon Cove) — "inherited" the new dwelling house on the island.

While the new construction and repairs to the old lighthouses went on, the Wheelers, one by one, moved on and off the island. Charles, the third Wheeler, however, became the victim of a political battle almost as soon as he assumed his duties as lightkeeper. That battle was to become even more intense than in Aaron's time, although some critics contended that his troubles were merely the results of his own incompetence.

In any case, the difficulties had actually started with Aaron Wheeler when Rufus Choate, a persuasive political figure, asked him to resign. Aaron, as noted earlier, refused to leave his post, and the political feud went on for many years, even up to the time Charles took over as lightkeeper in 1837.

Whether Charles deserved all the criticism heaped upon him remains a question. He had, in fact, some years earlier, had some difficulties with his own father. When his father, Moses Wheeler, died in 1824, the family farm (Garrison House) was divided among three sons, subject to the mother's dower rights. Moses' will provided that all was to go to her, but on her death the property was to be divided between John and Austin, while Charles and eight daughters were to receive fifty dollars each.

It is thought that Charles probably objected to being cut off, or possibly the family considered it unfair. In any case, on November 15, 1825, John, Austin, and their mother deeded a one-third interest to Charles; he was to relinquish his fifty-dollar legacy. In 1833 deeds were exchanged and the property was divided.

These were hard years for Charles Wheeler, as for all local fishermen. In 1839 two vessels and four lives were lost, the first ship near Thachers when the schooner *Sevo* was run down in the night by the steamer *Huntress,* and the *Sevo* sank immediately. Charles Wheeler was on hand, but without a serviceable boat he was unable to help the crew of either vessel.

Somehow, the captain of the *Sevo* was able to climb on board the steamer *Huntress* and was saved. Meanwhile, twelve-year-old Winthrop Sargent of Gloucester (on the *Sevo*) had managed to crawl out to the end of the bowsprit, and as the *Sevo* sank he grasped a floating board and yelled for help from the *Huntress*. Eventually, the sails of the *Sevo* drifted ashore, and Cape Anners were certain all hands from the *Sevo* had been lost, while the *Huntress*, with her two rescued men aboard, continued on her way. When the *Huntress* returned to Gloucester some time later, she discharged her passengers, and young Winthrop Sargent walked to town from the landing place at Eastern Point, much to the astonishment of his family, who had thought him lost with the *Sevo*.

That same year the schooner *Transport* was lost, but the entire crew was saved.

## Another Contract for Winslow Lewis

In the midst of the Wheeler family conflict with politicians, and a mere thirteen years after the repairs of 1828, a new contract was approved "to repair and refit the two lighthouses and lanterns on Thacher Island." And the contractor? The same Winslow Lewis, contractor for the keeper's house in 1816, and contractor for the Argand lamps in 1815, (including the seven-year maintenance program agreed upon by Lewis).

Again the contract was explicit. The old lanterns were now

*to be taken down to where the diameters measured 12 feet, then carried up perpendicular to their original height, the new wall to be laid with hard brick and to be carried up the same thickness as the stone walls where they commence. At the top of the walls a brick arch to be turned on which to be laid soapstone decks, 14 feet in diameter, well bedded in Roman cement, the outside circle of cement to be 4 inches thick and to be long enough to show 2 inches inside the lanterns. The lantern floor to be soapstone, on which to be wrought iron lanterns of sufficient height and diameter to admit in each octagon eight lights [panes] four by twenty inches, and two lights [panes] 24 by 12 inches with posts four inches wide and one inch thick to run down four feet into the walls. Sashes to show one fourth of an inch thick on the outside, rabbets one inch deep. The dome to be formed with 16 inch rafters, one inch iron, concentrating in an iron heap 7 inches wide and 12 inches diameter. In one of the octagons there is to be a door four feet by two feet to shut tight into rabbets, with two strong turn buttons.*

*On the top of the dome to be ventilators, 15 inches diameter, 27 inches high, an aperture on the side 12 by 6 inches. The funnel to project out 10 inches by 6 inches. The dome and doors to be covered with copper. The vanes which are to be 30 inches long and 12 inches wide to be covered with 28 ounce copper, round the lanterns to be an iron railing, railing posts 1 1/2 inch square, two rails seven inches square. Lanterns to be glazed with the best French plate glass of suitable thickness 24 by 20 inches; the lower sash 12 by 20 to be "fitted in" with 30 ounce copper, in four of which are to be ventilators. Lanterns to be painted two coats, outside black, inside white and the towers whitewashed. Each light house to be fitted up with ten lamps and ten 20 inch reflectors on two tiers. The reflectors to be formed on a die, each to be plated with fifteen ounces of pure silver, furnished with brass rims, two spare lamps, stove and funnel and the lamps fitted with oil heaters.*

A statement of completion and acceptance of the work, signed by Winslow Lewis, May 22, 1841, completed this government contract.

### A Year of Storms

Fortunately, the repair work on the island was finished early in the season, for 1841 was a year of disastrous storms. Little damage was reported from Thachers, but on the mainland Cape Anners suffered the full fury of one October blow. The storm struck with such force that it swept away the new breakwater in Rockport Harbor and then destroyed fourteen of the sixteen vessels in Pigeon Cove Harbor, these vessels representing the life savings and the livelihood of many Pigeon Cove fishermen.

Meanwhile, with all the repairs and reconstruction, with the constant calls for help from stricken vessels, and with the ongoing need for supplies to the island, the demand for a boat ramp had become increasingly urgent.

Eventually, a landing place was selected on the northwest side of the island at an upland, the only place on the island where a boat could land with reasonable safety. Markers had already been placed in holes in the rocks at this point in anticipation of the new boat ramp. The holes had been bored to be in sight at low tide, and one ledge here had been marked with a triangle from which to take bearings.

Between the markings already in place, stone was blasted and removed so that the bottom of the landing would be not less than five feet wide, and the rest of the landing not less than twelve feet wide and to "a sloping-off."

On August 13, 1842, William Hale Knowlton of Rockport signed the contract to clear away the rock and brush at this boatway site. Charles Wheeler, then in the lighthouse service for five years, approved the contract made with Levi Lincoln, port collector of Boston, and later superintendent of lighthouses in Massachusetts. Probably Charles Wheeler helped to complete the construction of the ramp. By September 30 the work was finished and approved, an essential addition to the work of Thachers that had waited seventy-five years. William Hale Knowlton received $225 for his labors, but some time passed before the island acquired a serviceable boat for Charles Wheeler to tie up on the new ramp.

## Charles Wheeler Clings to His Job

Charles Wheeler clung to his precarious job while Cape Ann storms matched the fury of his detractors. In May 1845 a disastrous four-day northeaster battered the island with loss of life as well as ships and cargoes. Heavy seas struck the schooner *Daniel Webster*, which was carrying a cargo of lumber from Ellsworth, Maine, to Boston. The vessel sprang a leak and drifted by Thachers toward Pebble Beach where it broke into pieces. The captain and the cook were washed overboard; a blind passenger was lost; and only one crewman was saved.

On the same day the schooner *Nicanor* from Bangor, Maine, passed Thachers in safety but, already in trouble, later went aground off Gloucester. The storm continued, becoming almost as destructive as the storm that took the *Watch and Wait* in 1635, and the next day Charles Wheeler risked his life to assist the *Royal Tar*.

After the shipwreck of the *Daniel Webster*, lighthouse engineers surveyed the Londoner once more and made two recommendations. They suggested that a beacon be placed on the rock, covered at high tide but visible as the tide ebbed about one-third, and they recommended that a lifeboat of moderate size be placed at the service of the keeper on Thachers in order to help anyone wrecked near the island.

## Charles Wheeler Continues His Fight

While the boatway was under construction, and for several years thereafter, criticisms of Charles Wheeler as keeper of the lights continued. Although, as mentioned, he gave aid to the *Royal Tar* that struck the Londoner and went down with a cargo of bricks on May 22, 1845, little mercy was shown him even when his wife died that same year. Nevertheless, he continued to fight for his job, as tenaciously as had Aaron Wheeler who preceded him. Finally, in self-defense, he took matters into his own hands. Placing a small basket in his dory, he rowed to Loblolly Cove and, carrying his basket with great care, took his case to the *Gloucester Telegraph and News*, where he found a sympathetic ear. On October 10, 1848, the newspaper published some words of support:

*Mr. Charles Wheeler, the keeper of Thacher Island lighthouses, has favored us with as fine a specimen of grapes as we have ever seen. They were raised by Mr. Wheeler on the island. Although almost isolated as it were from the world, he has devoted his leisure time to good and useful purpose.*

Six months later, during a January cold snap, Wheeler's publishing friends still remembered him. When the temperature in Gloucester fell below zero several times in a nine-day period, the newspaper reported that "the temperature on Thacher Island never once fell lower than one below!"

Severe weather continued into February that year, and during the first week of the month a sudden storm blew up a squall that endangered as many as 100 fishermen who had set out from the mainland as usual that day. When five boats failed to return, search parties were sent out and all returned in safety. Two made it to Thachers Island and sought shelter with Charles Wheeler.

## Charles Wheeler States His Case

Less than a year after Charles Wheeler took his prize grapes to Gloucester, he again felt it necessary to approach his friends at the Gloucester newspaper to plead for public understanding:

*I took charge of these lights Jan. 1, 1837, there was no person removed, my predecessor resigned. When I moved onto the island there was no fence, except a small garden fence about 50 feet square for which I paid my predecessor $30. There were no trees, bushes, roots or vines under cultivation, and the island was covered with Canada thistles. Since then, I have set out apples and pear trees, quince, currant and gooseberry bushes and blackberry, raspberry and grape vines all of which trees and bushes have arrived at maturity and for the last year or two I have had the happiness of sitting with my family and friends, under these trees and vines, and receiving the rich reward of my labors, by gathering the fruits. My children, also, have, for their amusements, cultivated a small flower garden, for which they have been highly praised and handsomely rewarded by the ladies and gentlemen who have visited the island during the flower season. I have cleared about two acres of land, and built about 140 rods [1 rod equals 5 1/2 to 8 yards] of stone wall, and 40 rods of wooden fence. I have got the island under a good state of cultivation, so that I have kept seven cows this year, and I have been for a year or two past, reaping the rewards of my hard labor. I have built and finished a neat and convenient milk room and I have floored over the large cellar — 33 feet square — with planks, and erected stands to set eleven oil butts upon. I have laid*

The stone wall built in the 1840s by Charles Wheeler.

platforms at the outside of the cellar doors and porch doors. I have furnished and set a good and convenient boiler in cellar. I have built and furnished a good and staunch brick porch over the eastern door of the dwelling house. I have put six iron braces upon the boat ways to secure them from being washed away in a heavy storm.

I have done most of the repairing required on the government boats here. I have done all the soldering and repairing of the lighthouse lamps for a number of years. I have built two banking walls at the south end of the dwelling and have wheeled in hundreds of wheelbarrow loads of rocks and dirt to level up to these walls, and to level around the house so as to make it look decent. I have built a good staunch hog pen, and a number of other small improvements I have not mentioned.

For all the above named improvements I have not received one cent for my labor, nor one cent for the money I have expended in accomplishing the work.

I have also invented and put to use, a good and useful lighthouse lamp, which saves the government not less than $30 per year. They have now been in use eleven years which has made a saving, in stoves and fuel, of not less than $300.

I have never received one cent of benefit from these lamps, except in labor, as it does not require one half the amount to keep them in order, *and to keep the lanterns neat and clean.*

*And the only recompense or thanks I received is the Secretary has been kind enough to notify me that my services are no longer required.*

*I have received thanks and the warmest expressions of gratitude from a great number of shipwrecked people who have been cast away here upon this island and Milk Island. Captain Robertson, of Schooner* Ann Maria, *even offered to give me his watch, the only thing saved by him or his crew except clothes on their backs. They were here three days, I took nothing from them. I made them all a small present and set them ashore, under a shower of thanks and expressions of gratitude to me, and to the Creator for their miraculous escape from a watery grave.*

*I also saved the lives of the crew of the* Fancy Packet *of Salem, Cap't Curtis, who were wrecked here about midnight in a northeast snow storm. At a very great risk of my own life, and that of my assistant keeper's. The greatest hazzard that I ever run of being drowned was in taking two men from the Schooner* Albany, *of Boston, that was cast away upon Milk Island. I performed this task in my wherry. I have boarded and assisted vessels in distress, and should have done more if government had given me a suitable boat.*

*There have been a great many of our wherry fishermen who have been caught out in thick foggy weather and squalls who have no other retreat but to this island; and I feel justified in saying that they were comfortably provided for during their stay upon this island, and for which I have received their kind wishes and thanks. They all offered me money, but I never was guilty of taking one cent from a distressed, shipwrecked person.*

*I only wish it was in my power to find words to express my gratitude to my influential Whig friends of Gloucester and Rockport for volunteering their services to retain me on the island, but I have been so shamefully abused for the 12 years past, that I do not wish to be retained here any longer. Gentlemen, receive my kindest thanks, it is the only means that I have of rewarding you.*

*Charles Wheeler*
*Keeper of Thacher Island Lights*


Charles Wheeler's touching defense came too late, for William Hale took charge of the lighthouses on August 9, 1849, having already received his official appointment in June.

In spite of all the critics said, Charles did in fact rescue the crew of the *Ann Maria* on a stormy January 21 in 1837, as he had said. He did assist the crews of the *Fancy Packet* and the *Albany*, and he probably did experiment with the lights. He was also on hand to give help when the schooner *President* was lost off Thachers Island on September 15, 1848. His political problems may, in fact, have been the least of his hardships. His ailing wife had died of "gravel," and Charles was left with five sons and two daughters. Of obvious necessity he still clung to his post.

Some years later he published his intentions to marry again, but a scant few months after his dismissal from lighthouse tending, the work he so tenaciously held on to, he departed for California with other Cape Ann men to seek a fortune in gold. Offers of lightkeepers' salaries of $1,000 may have tempted him, too, while West Coast lightkeepers went on to pan for gold themselves. Evidently Charles had no more luck in finding gold or in doubling his salary than had Aaron Wheeler and Ebenezer Pool on Thachers. Charles wrote home to his children a letter of nostalgia in which he told them that otters and beavers were "as plenty as the fish round Thachers Island." Yet another letter contained some verses written either by Charles or by one of his sons who accompanied him to California. With thoughts of their former island home, one of them penned some poignant verses of their leavetaking;

> *Farewell, old house, a sad farewell*
> *Farewell, farewell, my island home.*

# 1849–1853

*C*HARLES WHEELER claimed that he invented the new lens. Possibly he did, but it is more probable that he experimented with Winslow Lewis and tried out the new lens and reflectors in both the north and the south towers.

Yet another French inventor, Augustin Fresnel, who had been working since 1822, had persisted with his lens and had worked hours on end to perfect it for seacoast lighting. This lens was already in advance of anything in use but still had not reached the United States.

Fresnel had developed seven "orders," or sizes, of lenses, the first order being the largest. The importance of Thachers called for a first order lens,* though early lights were probably no more than third- or fourth-order ones.

It was a long time, however, before this lens, so far in advance of anything being used in the United States, reached this side of the Atlantic. Designed to look somewhat like a beehive in shape—"a giant beehive that surrounded a single lamp,"—the prisms at top and bottom refracted the light into a narrow sheet so that it magnified the light many times.

When information about the Fresnel lens eventually reached the United States, the out-of-date Argands came under severe criticism. Inevitably, critics began to question the business practices of Winslow Lewis and the ethics of his friend in Washington, Stephen Pleasonton, the fifth auditor

---

* In recent years one of these first-order lenses was removed from the south tower at Thachers, its 174 pieces of glass packed with care, and stored in thirty cartons at the Coast Guard Academy Library at New London, Connecticut.

at the Treasury Department. Ironically, their sternest critic was I. W. P. Lewis, nephew of Winslow!

The nephew asserted that his uncle helped prepare the specifications for the new lighthouses, then bid on the jobs himself, invariably obtaining the contracts. "Favoritism showed," he claimed, "if not absolute dishonesty."

"The relationship," said Francis Ross Holland, Jr., in *American Lighthouses*, "was perhaps between a sharp but honest Yankee and an uninformed government bureaucrat." In any case, it was widely recognized that Pleasonton "did a lot of footdragging."

As fifth auditor, Pleasonton was in charge of the lighthouse service for the government, but his interest was in saving money rather than in maintaining the lighthouses for public safety. He therefore accepted Lewis's recommendations without question because he possessed the practical marine experience that Pleasonton lacked.

Meanwhile, the nephew criticized not only his uncle and Pleasonton but the entire lighthouse service. As a result of all this criticism, which focused public attention on the lighthouse service, Congress ordered an investigation into all aspects of the service and aids to navigation.

Such an investigation, too long delayed, found nothing at all to commend within the lighthouse service. So harsh, in fact, were the Congressional committee's criticisms — use of poorly constructed lanterns, of chimneys that were too short, of too many wicks (even then inadequate) and, in addition, that "Keepers lacked training and in general did not know how to tend the lights" — that Congress responded with immediate action.

First, it moved to provide a lighthouse board to administer these aids to navigation rather than leaving the work to the fifth auditor. Then it began to reorganize the entire lighthouse system, setting in motion a plan for regular and frequent inspections. Finally, with inspections under way, things began to improve, and at the same time so much pressure reached Pleasonton that he agreed to experiment with the lens so long pushed aside, the Fresnel lens.

By this time, the new board of administrators had found to be only too true that almost no instruction was offered the keepers on how to tend the lights. Some light stations were simply not well kept because no instructions whatever were available when a new keeper assumed his duties.

At one time, after the nephew Lewis had openly voiced disapproval, an instruction sheet made the rounds of the light stations, in a halfhearted attempt to convey instructions, but many lightkeepers claimed that they never received the sheet of instructions. Sometimes an outgoing keeper

The north tower before the 1981 restoration.

offered some "hit-or-miss" training before he left, but for the most part new keepers taught themselves the essentials of keeping the lights going.

## Conversion to Fresnel Lens

As soon as the new lighthouse board got organized, the situation did a complete turnaround. No time was lost in converting the entire system of lighthouses to the use of the Fresnel lens.

Congress had already sent Comdr. Matthew Perry to France to buy two Fresnel lamps, one first-order fixed lens and one second-order revolving lens. It took an act of Congress to get them installed, but by 1860 all the old Argands had been dismantled and all the lighthouses had the new Fresnels in use,* with two exceptions.

By 1859 the twin lighthouses of Thachers and the lighthouse at Cape Canaveral, Florida, were the only lights left without the new Fresnel lighting equipment. Since the twins were, by this time, undergoing the construction of new stone towers, the work of installing the Fresnels was delayed there until the towers were completed. Meanwhile, the Canaveral lights were installed, making Thachers the last light station in the United States to retain the outdated reflector apparatus, the Argand.

## Minor Repairs

The friction caused by political favoritism had stirred feelings on Thachers Island for almost fifty years, but with the departure of the Wheelers and the adoption of the Fresnel lamps, William Hale assumed without fanfare the post of keeper of the Thachers Island lights. He held the post until 1853 and even the repairs during his term of service appear to have been minor ones.

During his first year of service he reported to inspectors: "The towers have been whitewashed inside and out and the doors and lanterns painted and in good order." He also hung a new chandelier and brass lamps in the south tower. "Reflectors are good," he reported, "and there are new burners to the lamps in the north lighthouse."

With the improved lighthouse system at work, and working well, public attention focused more and more on the work of the twin sentinels and their warnings of the treacherous rocks.

Still, vessels continued to founder around Thachers. On April 8, 1850, a large topsail schooner, "bound east and going nine miles an hour," struck

---

* One hundred years later these Fresnels were still in use, but electric bulbs had replaced the oil lamps used during the Civil War period, and in the 1970s the Coast Guard installed an "airplane-type" beacon.

the schooner *Anti*, which was loaded with a cargo of sand. The *Anti* sank about 9:00 P.M. abreast of Thachers, but the crew took refuge on the island, and Captain Hale and his wife gave them food, clothing, and lodging.

One year later the British brig *Hope* struck the Londoner in a November storm, drifted off, and later sank. The following year, again in a November storm, the *Frances* collided with the schooner *Bloomer* one mile east of Thachers.

During the four years the Hales lived on Thachers, political differences gave way to the real-life drama of lifesaving, but not many years were to elapse before politics would affect the island again. Meanwhile, the island approached a new era. With the departure of the Hales and the appointment of a new lightkeeper, the Thachers Island Light Station moved inevitably toward the up-to-date system of lights for which it had waited so long.

# 1853–1860

*J*N 1853 Lancelot Kelly Rowe succeeded William Hale as keeper of
the Thacher lights. At age 33, he
rowed in his dory to his new job on Thachers, and another brief period
of peace settled over the island.

Unlike the keepers who had preceded him, most of whom were
mariners, Lancelot was a painter — of both houses and pictures. After performing his lighthouse service, his passion for colors and artistic form in-
spired him to clip and tailor the garden that surrounded his home at Joppa, and he painted a number of canvases of this scene. He so loved color
that, when his neighbors hired him to paint their houses, he was known
to paint door panels in three different colors, to the delight of some but
to the dismay of others with more conservative tastes.

On the island there was no end to the painting to be done — the woodwork in the twin towers and the interior of the dwelling house. In his new
job, however, Rowe found some of the leisure he sought to practice the
painting of pictures as well, and his subjects ranged from wildflowers to
lighthouses.

While Rowe painted and tended the lights, so much a part of his work-
day, travelers were beginning to notice and to be curious about the island.
In 1853 Henry David Thoreau sailed by, noticed the lights of Thachers,
and recorded in his journal: "Now we see the Cape Ann lights, and now
pass near a small village-like fleet of mackerel fishers at anchor, probably
off Gloucester."

That same year an agent for the Portland Steam Packet Company,

Primitive painting of his home at Joppa by Lightkeeper Lancelot Rowe.

traveling by Thachers on his regular sailing schedule, called to the attention of the lighthouse inspector, Lieutenant Franklin of Boston, the "need for a suitable bell to be placed on Thacher Island, Cape Ann, to be rung during periods of fog." Not only were his own shipping interests at stake, but lives were threatened, and he pointed out that "this island and its twin lights are the keys to Boston Harbor."

The bell was duly installed, and that same year Lancelot and his wife, Nancy Beal Rowe, acquired a second daughter, to whom they gave the name Belle Thacher.*

### The Londoner Beacon Repaired at Great Risk

The new fog bell not only helped to save lives and ships but also directed public attention to the lighthouse service. At the same time, it served as an opening wedge toward replacing the old 45-foot towers with new and taller ones.

Long before discussions about new towers began in Washington, though, there were more immediate repairs to be attended to close by the island. In 1852 two beacons placed on the Londoner had both been washed away. Workmen were making an effort to replace them, but it was to be a frustrating three years before these important navigational aids could function.

---

* Two great-grand-daughters, Ethel Publicover Howard and Mildred Anderson Olson, live in Gloucester, and the late Helen Poole Church, of Rockport, was a granddaughter.

This ledge of rock, southeast of Thachers, was still considered one of the most dangerous along the coast. At low tide about one acre was visible, but at high tide or during rough weather there was little protection from this hazard. Since the loss of the beacons, workmen tried unsuccessfully to replace a shaft for a new beacon on this rock, but they faced extreme handicaps. They could work only in fair weather, at lowest tide, and with a smooth sea — and then only for a short time. The wrought-iron shaft, stored at Rockport, was 45 feet long and 23 inches in diameter at its base, and 5 inches at the top. It weighed thirteen tons.

For this formidable project, a five-foot-deep hole had to be shaped into the rock, and for the tip of the shaft an iron framework had to be cast, 6 feet long and 15 inches in diameter.

Work went on under these difficult conditions for two years, until at last everything seemed in readiness to raise the shaft. With all precautions taken, the shaft was placed in a vessel and transported to the Londoner, but there the workmen faced the almost impossible task of raising the extremely heavy shaft. The seas rocked the boat, causing the tremendous weight of the shaft to threaten to capsize it, so that the workmen were forced to drop the shaft. When it fell, the tip of the shaft broke off.

This discouraging development resulted in a decision to go place the shaft in the hole anyway. Repairs could be made later, it was thought, but a year later efforts were still being made to raise the shaft. By the end of August 1855, the tip had at last been repaired and the framework placed around it — and this time the weather cooperated and the beacon was finally erected.

With the completion of this work on the Londoner's beacon, and also of the placing of the fog bell, the first official recommendation was then made "to refit the lens apparatus in the two towers on Thacher Island, off Cape Ann Point, Massachusetts." (This recommendation also applied to the Boston Light on Little Brewster Island at the entrance to Boston Harbor.) These two locations were the only ones that were considered "first-class light stations" and thus deserving of this specific modernization.

## Talk of New Towers Begins

The time had come to think about building some new towers.
Coast Guard officials reported in 1857:

*The two lighthouse towers at Cape Ann are only 45 feet high each; built of very inferior materials, badly constructed, and require attention, especially during the season of winter storms, to keep them in a fit condition for the exhibition of the lights.*

*The character of the shore and water of Cape Ann is more bold and broken than any thus far surveyed. The shores are bold and abrupt. There are dangerous ledges and rocks off the eastern point of the Cape, the "Salvages," and the Londoner, but the lights of Thachers are sufficient guides to navigators in avoiding them.*

The lights, in fact, served as day markers as well as night markers, something that was often overlooked.

Pressing its case, the survey committee assured government officials that the

*Boston and Cape Ann lights occupy a prominent position, with many dangers to the navigator, of about two thirds of the circle around them. It is believed that the interests of commerce and navigation would be greatly benefited by having two lights of the First Order in place of the present ones; and that it would be a wise economy to substitute the lens apparatus whenever Congress may think proper to make the necessary appropriation for rebuilding them, the estimation of cost for which is $68,751.*

Following this recommendation, made in 1858, temporary repairs were made on both the Boston Light and the lighthouse towers at Cape Ann. The repairs were temporary, apparently, because the recommendation and the urgent need to replace the now nearly 100-year-old lighthouses had already reached Congress for consideration.

Congress eventually approved the plans for the new towers, to be built " of cut granite," for Thachers Island. The towers were under construction for nearly two years, with the date of completion promised for 1861. The contract, to the dismay of many Cape Anners, called for the stone to be brought from Concord, New Hampshire, even though the granite industry at Cape Ann was at its height. Concord granite, it was decided, was softer and thus easier to cut, and the round towers called for special cutting and shaping, but Cape Anners protested vehemently.

## Construction of the Towers, 1859-61

Although Cape Ann granite was prized as well as praised for its firm texture, freedom from impurities, and ability to withstand various crushing tests, for the above-mentioned reason — and perhaps for a number of other reasons — it was not selected for use in the construction of the twin towers. As to the true reasons, there can be only speculation, for many records have been destroyed.

The contract for stone went to Concord, New Hampshire, granite quarries, although it is possible that some or all of the stone was transported by barge from Chelmsford or Westford quarries, which were not as far from Thachers. In any case, the transportation problems would have been similar, whether the granite came from these quarries or from Concord.

If, indeed, some of the stone was transported from Concord, it would have first been cut in the New Hampshire quarries, then hauled by oxen to the Merrimack River and transported by barge down the river to Lowell, Massachusetts, where a barge loaded with stone would have traveled through the Middlesex Canal, on through Chelmsford, the thirty miles to Boston, and from there up and down the coast to shipping points.

If this was the actual route of the stone used for building the twin towers of Thachers, for Cape Anners it was an unhappy circumstance. Yet there was another possibility that angered Cape Anners even more, and it stirred them to oppose by public letter the use of any stone except that from the Cape Ann quarries.

Sydney Perley was a Cape Ann writer long interested in Cape Ann happenings, and at this time especially in the construction of the stone towers. In February 1859, when word of building the towers had only begun to circulate, Perley reported in a local newspaper:

*Gloucester gentlemen are urging an appropriation for rebuilding the lighthouses at Thacher Island at Cape Ann, and furnishing them with First Class illuminating apparatus, at a cost of $81,417. The rebuilding of these lights is much needed and I am happy to learn that Senator Clay, Chairman of the Senate Committee, has withdrawn his opposition.*

Even with men such as Perley as champions of the cause, the final congressional signature had "hung fire," and Cape Ann waited eagerly for the results. Now, with the contract at last awarded to the Swenson Quarries of Concord, New Hampshire, Cape Anners were less than happy as they contemplated use of anything but their own admired Cape Ann granite.

In December of that same year, Perley again wrote of the towers and their construction, and this time he wrote also of the indignation over proposed use of "outside" granite.

"The good people of Cape Ann," Perley wrote, "are proud of their granite and are quite indignant at learning that the contractor for rebuilding the lighthouses on Thacher Island proposes to use Chelmsford stone."*

* In an effort to identify the granite used in the Thachers Island lighthouses, Walter Johnson of Pigeon Cove compared the stone with that taken from the Swenson Quarries in Concord, New Hampshire, and he declared them to be identical.

According to Perley, Cape Ann officials submitted samples of their granite to be compared with Chelmsford stone (considered by some to be somewhat softer than Cape Ann stone). At that time, Quincy granite apparently had a reputation as yet unachieved by Rockport, and many claimed to use Quincy granite when it actually was cut at other quarries. Rockport had, nevertheless, already furnished stone for lighthouses at Pensacola, Florida, and at Mobile, Alabama.

Then, eighteen months after Perley's report, in June 1860, again he wrote, making only slight concession to the construction materials, "Preparations are being made, and the work of rebuilding the two lighthouses on Thachers Island has already been commenced. The new structures will no doubt be of substantial build and in every way suitable for the purposes designed."

One week later, however, politics continued to hassle the project and swirl about the island. A letter appeared in the *Salem Register* calling attention of voters to the construction of the towers and referring to them as "the government work now in progress."

The writer stated:

*The lighthouses at Thacher Island are to be rebuilt, and one would suppose that the Rockport quarries, which are close at hand, would be enabled to furnish the granite with the most facility and cheaper. But that is not always the way of doing things under this economical administration.* *
*It is said that the contract has been given to somebody in Quincy and sublet to another, who procures the material in Chelmsford, where it is transported in the rough to Lowell and there dressed. Thence by railroad to Salem, thence by water to Thacher Island. Rockport quarries are within an hour's sail of the location of these lights. How much is saved by this governmental operation? Facts in the case have a curious look.*

Although the questions went unanswered, interest of Cape Anners and visitors remained high as the construction continued. One further possibility for not choosing Cape Ann stone presented itself. In 1857-58 Rockport and Lanesville quarries employed 300 men with "large contracts." It is possible they were too busy to provide the stone for the time these government contracts called for completion, for at that time some workers were also on strike.

In any case, by August 1860 the original old towers had been removed and temporary lights installed while the stonework went on. At this time

---

* The administration of President James Buchanan.

the *Boston Journal* reported that "French" (Fresnel) lenses had been purchased by the government at a cost of $10,000 each and that the new lighthouses would measure 30 feet in diameter at the base. "As the walls rise," the article went on, "courses of heavy stone are laid two feet thick, gradually diminishing upward to the lantern deck where the lantern lessens to 18 feet."

The massive stone walls described in the article enclosed yet another wall of brick, 2 feet thick, with a space of 18 inches between brick and stone. Architects made the walls round to resist both wind and wave, a design that caused heavy seas to fall back if they struck the towers.

With the work well along, the latest report on the stonework claimed that it had been cut at Weston quarries and that the contract for the heavy masonry had been awarded to the Boston firm of Adams and Roberts.

The work had begun in April, and James Collins Parsons was the current lighthouse keeper. Both structures were expected to be completed by fall. Contractor Roberts superintended the project, and he lived on the island as the work progressed.

The name of the architect for the twin towers remains a mystery. It is known that a talented Boston architect, Gridley James Fox Bryant, then in his prime at age forty-two, had designed hundreds of stone buildings in Boston and for the United States government, including post offices, schoolhouses, and customhouses, in addition to the famous Minot's Light, just then completed in 1859.

For the Minot's Light contract, Lt. Col. B. S. Alexander was assigned the construction by the chief engineer of the U.S. Army, General Totten, then also a member of the lighthouse board. It is possible that he was also assigned the work at Thachers, since it followed immediately the work on Minot's Light.

Curiosity remains to this day as to methods of cutting and transporting to this island the great pieces of granite more than 100 years ago. Thanks to one man, Almoran Holmes, progress in handling the heavy stone was well under way in 1860, for Holmes had long been at work seeking a satisfactory lifting device for the stoneworkers.

The first crude method of handling granite was by hand (in the manner of Aaron and Charles Wheeler as well as James Kirkwood before them); then the granite blocks were moved on to shipping points by oxen; later on, by railroad. The first 45-foot towers on Thachers (1771) had been "laid up" with handpower and oxen, with wood ferried from the mainland and fieldstone found on the island.

Within a few decades, however, Holmes had invented the lifting device known as the Holmes hoist, and Thachers Island lighthouses benefited from this important development.

Steampower, too, had been in use for a few years. The *Gloucester Telegraph and News* reported that an engine had been attached to a former windlass. Admirers asserted that it took no more room than a "molasses truncheon," and "it can be run," they said, "with small expense." Initial cost of this invention was $500, but a single man could work the engine and tend the "purchase fall" at the same time. "Onward," they proclaimed in May 1858, "is the march of progress."

All this, of course, came as engineering windfall for the Thachers Island project.

Holmes, who was possessed of great engineering skills, had been a practical seaman as well. He had spent years studying the lifting and hoisting of granite in the quarries and was particularly skillful in the use of the rope "purchases" such as were required for swinging great blocks of stone onto this island. Although Holmes died in an accident in 1834, his hoisting device was a remarkable machine, considered "easy" and "graceful," terms rarely used to describe machinery.

The device had an arm capable of swinging in a 50-foot circle (i.e., a circle 100 feet in diameter). It could lift a weight and land it "gracefully" at any point on the circumference, at the foot of a derrick. It was also useful for storing and reloading material. "It left nothing to be desired," users claimed, "in the way of lifting the heavy stone."

Other machines — a lifting jack for turning over the heavy blocks of stone and a pulling jack for carting and hauling stone out of the quarries — were also in use, all of these with a power of about ten tons weight.

All that summer of 1860 the work of building the twin towers went on; completion of the work was promised for fall, which was none too soon — two schooners had already been lost off Thachers that year.

By the time the towers were completed the cost had soared to $80,000, but the towers were considered "first class in every respect." The new lights, 163 feet above sea level, were visible 25 miles away in clear weather. (For stormy weather, the long-delayed fog warning was installed at this time. A powerful fog whistle — steam — now warned vessels of the dangers at hand.)

By the end of July a "Notice to Mariners" went out — number 3 in its history — from the lighthouse board:

*Notice is hereby given that the two stone lighthouse towers, which have been under construction for some time on Thacher's Island, distant about*

# NOTICE TO MARINERS.

## (No. 3.)

---

# CAPE ANN, MASSACHUSETTS.

*Two Gray-colored Stone Towers, and Two First Order Fixed Lights,*

## ON THATCHER'S ISLAND.

---

Notice is hereby given that the two stone light-house towers which have been for some time under construction on "Thatcher's Island," distant about three-fourths of a mile from Cape Ann, (which forms the northernmost limit to Massachusetts Bay,) will be completed, and the lights exhibited for the first time on the evening of the 1st day of October, 1861.

The illuminating apparatus of each light is *first order catadioptric* for fixed

---

Third Notice to Mariners in the history of the Coast Guard issued on July 29, 1861.

three fourths of a mile from Cape Ann, which forms the northeastern-most limit of Massachusetts Bay, will be completed, and the lights exhibited for the first time, on the evening of the first day of October, 1861.

The notice went on to describe the towers:

The two towers are built of gray granite: the lanterns and parapet railings are painted red; the work rooms and covered walks attached to the towers are painted stone color; the keeper's dwelling for the north tower is a frame building two stories in height, and is painted white; that for the south tower is brick (red) and is two and one half stories in height.

*The height of each tower from base to focal plane is 112 1/2 feet, and the height of each focal plane above the mean sea level is 165 1/2 feet. They occupy the positions of the old stone towers at the distance of 298 yards from each other. There is a good channel between Thacher's Island and Cape Ann for small vessels.*

The towers were equipped with Fresnel first-order fixed lens and oil-wick lamps.

While Cape Anners followed the progress of building the stone towers with concern and high interest, they also focused their attention on two other events of significance far beyond the limits of one small island.

In November 1860 Rockporters overwhelmingly voted to elect Abraham Lincoln as president of the United States; closer to home, the Gloucester-Rockport branch of the Eastern Railroad opened for travel only one month after the new lights went on in the 124-foot stone towers on Thachers Island.

# 1860-1868

*C*ONSTRUCTION of the stone towers had continued on the island for two years. Meanwhile, James Collins Parsons, with his wife, Mary Ann, replaced Lancelot Rowe as keeper, having as assistants William H. Tarr, James C. Parsons, Jr., and Benjamin Parsons, Jr. With the completion of the towers, however, Albert Giddings Hale, born in 1813, was appointed to keep the new lights in order during most of the Civil War period.

Although some of the earlier lightkeepers had been appointed because of their particular maritime skills, and others were political appointees, Hale, at age forty-eight, went to Thachers, somewhat reluctantly, for his health. He had only partially recovered from a bout with typhoid fever, and when the opening as keeper was offered, his doctor advised him to take the job for a year to try to regain his health.

Hale's family was as reluctant as he was to move from the mainland to Thachers, but there were five children — two boys and three girls — and this was a way to provide for them while Albert regained his strength. The family moved to the island by way of dories, and to their surprise life on the island was anything but dull. Albert's wife, Mary Choate Blatchford Hale, was a lively and sociable woman. She had participated with her five sisters in the famed (Hannah Jumper) Rockport liquor raid of 1856,[*] and was never one to sit on the sidelines when action came along. Friends and relatives of the Hales came to Thachers by the boatload to visit them, and there were parties and good times as often as weather per-

---

[*] See *Hannah and the Hatchet Gang* by Eleanor C. Parsons, 1975.

Albert Giddings Hale, lightkeeper from 1861 to 1864 and his wife Mary Choate Blatchford Hale, participant in Hannah Jumper's raid of 1856.

mitted rowboats to reach them. For as long as the Hales were there, they seldom lacked for excitement.

Only a few months before the Hales moved to the island, the *S.S. Eastern City* had come upon five humpback whales off Cape Ann, and they were still visible from time to time. They were marine monsters in their mating season, and the steamship struck the largest of the herd — sixty feet long — with such force that the impact damaged the ship to the extent that it had to be dry-docked at East Boston for repairs. Two days later another whale threatened and narrowly missed a passing steamship.

On the mainland, 1861 was "a sickly year" according to historian Ebenezer Pool, and one woman, he claimed, was "suicidicle." In addition to a rash of epidemics, no less than five schooners were lost in the vicinity of Thachers.

At one time a great northeast gale drove three coasting vessels onto the island, one after another, but with the aid of the Hales and their assistants (Eben Abbott was one) all the crews were rescued.

In December a violent northwest gale drove the 140-ton schooner *Gypsee* onto Thachers. Again, with the help of keeper Hale and his assistants, all crew members were saved. Earlier, the 70-ton schooner *Pierce* had been driven ashore on Thachers. Although the crews were saved, both vessels were destroyed. Hale was called upon to assist the survivors of all these shipwrecks.

At yet another time, an escaped prisoner of war was recaptured in a rowboat near Thachers. He had rowed from Boston and was on his way to freedom in Canada.

The Civil War was not yet over when the Hale family moved back to the mainland — as reluctantly as they had gone to Thachers in the first place. Alexander Bray, a Civil War veteran recovering from his wounds, took over as lightkeeper at a salary of $1,000. The salary of $1,000 was probably divided among the assistants and the principal keeper, although it may have included a raise or a bonus for Bray's Civil War service.

## Heroics: Alexander and Maria Bray

Among the many heroic men and women who have lived on Thachers, Maria and Alexander Bray stand out as having a special kind of courage. While most wives of the keepers faced the prospect of great loneliness on the island, Maria looked forward with enthusiasm to this new experience with Alexander. They had been married for six years, during which time Alexander had served in the Civil War. After his service, like his predecessor, he needed to regain his health, and he assumed the duties of lighthouse keeper on the island, first as assistant, then as principal keeper.

Maria, like Mary Hale before her, was sociable and lively, and her friends gasped in horror at the thought of Maria living in "that desolate place." The thirty-three-year-old Maria, however, looked upon the experience as a privilege. "It will be a rough sea that will keep me ashore," she assured her friends, "and as far as that goes, I can pull an oar with the best of them."

During their first summer on Thachers, the schooner *Gazette*, carrying a cargo of coal, went aground on the Londoner on July 24, 1864, but this was merely a forerunner of what was to come.

While Alexander tended the lights and cleared more of the brush and rock that James Kirkwood and Charles Wheeler had started to clear, Maria explored the island. The wildness of the surf, rolling over the rocks and flinging mist in her face, filled her with excitement. She studied the rocks with the eagerness of a trained geologist, and she gathered sea mosses and marine algae for study, for drying and pressing, and for making artistic arrangements. In addition, she learned from Alexander how to clean the lights, trim the wicks, and fill the oil pans.

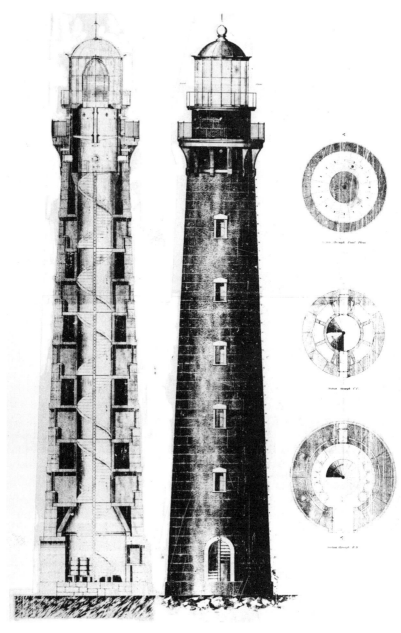

Vertical and horizontal sections and front elevation of "Light House for Cape Ann, Mass." by Capt. W. B. Franklin, Engineer.

Maria never hesitated to set off alone in a boat to catch fresh fish and was known to have caught codfish, return to her island dwelling, clean the fish, and make codfish chowder.

"She took in the length and breadth of a situation," said a friend, "and made herself mistress of all its resources."

It was inevitable that Maria one day would have a chance to prove her courage and go to the limits of her resources. Her opportunity came on December 21, 1864, by coincidence the ninety-third anniversary date of lighting the towers for the first time in 1771. (The new stone towers were but three years old.)

One of the two assistants became ill with a high fever, and the home remedies Maria offered had little effect on him. His temperature continued to rise, and Alexander decided that someone must get him to a doctor and to his family on the mainland. Alexander thus set off without delay, taking with him another assistant to watch over the ailing man as well as to help load some needed oil and provisions.

That day a light southwest wind sent scarcely a ripple over Sandy Bay, but within two hours the wind shifted to the southeast, dark clouds foretold stormy weather, and by two o'clock in the afternoon so much snow had fallen that visibility between the mainland and the island was cut off. By the time Alexander had obtained medical attention for the sick man and left him in the care of his family, he realized that any attempt to row back to the island would be futile. He and his assistant sought shelter for the night.

Meanwhile, Maria and fourteen-year-old Sidney Haskell (Maria's nephew) waited with the greatest anxiety for the safe return of the men.

As the storm's intensity increased, and with darkness setting in by three o'clock, Maria knew what she must do. Fearful as she was for the safety of her husband, who for all she knew was struggling to make his way back across the bay in a rowboat, Maria and Sidney headed for the south tower.

The covered passageway gave them temporary shelter from the gale-force winds but no relief whatever from the intense cold. It was with numbed fingers that Maria and Sidney prepared the south tower lights, as Alexander had taught them — cleaning the glass of the Fresnel lamps and filling the containers with oil.

Then, with the wind still thundering around them, the two descended the spiral stairs, slammed shut the heavy iron door, and faced into the driving snow toward the north tower, 300 yards distant. Maria leaned her weight into the second iron door, pushed it open and out of breath from her exertions, dropped onto one of the stone benches near the door.

Sidney, shivering with the cold, rested on another stone bench along the opposite wall.

This first-floor room, as cold as any iceberg, was a circular stone cell, 15 feet high and 15 feet across, the top half tapering toward the stairway. Aware that their work was only half done, the two began their climb.

The twenty-five steps they climbed to the first landing were almost a relief after their struggle through wind and snow. On this first landing, it would have been futile to peer out of the window of the alcove, for snow beat wildly against the thick glass, completely shutting them inside.

Twenty steps to the second landing. Already their snow boots and ankle-length storm coats felt too heavy.

Another twenty steps to the third landing. Here the alcoves were somewhat smaller, closing them in a grip even tighter than before.

Twenty steps to the fourth landing. Here the alcoves narrowed to a width of three feet.

Twenty steps to the fifth landing. Here the alcoves extended only 2½ feet.

By this time, the frigid air had cut their breathing to gasps, while the higher they climbed the louder the wind howled, clutching at their weary minds and defying their senses.

Twenty-four steps to the sixth landing. Here four portholes, each 18 inches wide, normally mirrored an unconfined view of the Atlantic. Now, however, no thought of the view entered their consciousness as they plodded upward. In what seemed a madhouse of cold stone to Maria, her lantern cast its eerie shadows along the side wall to a ladder-type stairway.

Ten more steps led to yet another room, 6 feet high, directly below the lens room. Here six air shafts battled the wind with a roar more deafening than ever.

Nine steps now remained, in a step-ladder arrangement, leading up to the lens room.

Maria climbed to the lens room, Sidney stumbling behind her, giving her little help except by his presence. They had climbed one hundred and forty-eight steps! The lens room, 10 feet high, contained forty-eight panes of glass (now replaced with plexiglass) that surrounded the lens. Maria wiped the smoke from these panes as best she could, somehow trimmed off the soot with her chilled fingers, and refilled the oil pans.

Three times during the night, Maria repeated this superhuman feat, climbing each tower and keeping the lights going by means of a clockwork arrangement that pumped the oil for five hours, then had to be refilled.

Waves churned up by the storm pounded the shores of the island and the mainland for two days while the sick man recovered at his home. From time to time, Alexander and his worried assistant peered at the island, the assistant asking the same question over and over: "How many ships will be lost without attention to the lights?"

"Never fear," Alexander reassured him. "Maria can manage the lights."

His confidence in his wife's ability never failed, and Alexander and his assistant returned to the island at dawn of the third day of the storm. The lights still burned and the exhausted Maria was sound asleep.

"Maria, you are a brave woman," was all Alexander could say as he wakened his wife, but the Christmas star joined the twin lights that Christmas morning to make it probably the happiest Christmas ever celebrated on Thachers.

(The valiant Maria lived to be ninety-three and died in 1921, much loved and mourned.)

The Brays remained on the island for almost five years. The next twelve years saw Joseph Wingood, Michael Dundon, and Albert William Hale (son of Albert Giddings Hale) come and go as lighthouse keepers. During these years it must have seemed that everything on the island needed repairs.

Maria Bray had proved the new lights which had replaced those "hither-to of very inferior quality, power, and range," to be successful. Yet, there was a never-ending need for repair of these as well as all other buildings on the island.

Within five years, the keeper's house required a storage closet, the house pump was repaired, and the watch room call bell was hung with iron and cranks. Outside, the path from the boat landing was widened to permit passage of a small cart to carry supplies for the towers and the fog signal. A new stone floor was laid in the enginehouse, and an adjoining coalshed was built.

## Boatway and Other Repairs

The next year (1868) it was time to repair the boatway, built some twenty-five years earlier. In addition to these changes, the keeper and his assistants enlarged the cistern of the new dwelling, retopped the chimney, reset the ventilator, enlarged the woodshed, resurfaced the roof, and reshingled the sides. Weather was taking its usual great toll of buildings on the island. Repairs on the outside of these buildings were even more demanding than those in the interiors. It was necessary to repaint the walls, to reshingle the old stone house, to repair the boat, and to procure a new compass as well as new stove fixtures and lamp covers. At this time, the

The walkway from the boathouse and ramp to the dwellings as it appears today.

scow that had been used to bring the fog signal engine had been redecked, and the cistern and oil butt had been recovered with boards.

In addition to all these repairs, a partition was built in the attic of the wooden house, near the north tower, in order to make a clothes press. Added to this, all the equipment for the lights was examined; burners were repaired; and the interiors of both towers were repainted, along with the exterior of the wooden dwelling — two coats of paint for all. The keepers also provided, painted, and hung thirty-seven sets of window blinds and trimmings for both houses, supplied two new cistern pumps, and wallpapered one room and two entryways.

As if this were not enough repair work for one year, three times — in April, July, and September — they repaired and repacked the fog signal that had been installed in 1859.

# 1868–1902

THE STONE TOWERS were bare-ly eight years old in 1869, but the Cape Ann Light Station edged toward its one hundredth birthday. At this time, even the new stonework needed an overhaul. While the pointing up of loose mortar proceeded, renovations inside included a lathed and plastered partition between the two kitchens of the north dwellling to replace the simple, ancient wooden partition. A new iron sink soon graced each kitchen; the woodwork was repainted and wallpaper was supplied, to be hung by the keeper and his wife. Outside improvements, besides the mortarwork, were acquisition of a new boat, a new ensign, and a new oil-burner carrier.

Inspectors, mostly Army and Navy personnel, now examined the lighting apparatus on a regular schedule. Following one such inspection, they ordered the tinware and carillon repaired, a lens stack made, and wick rings supplied.

As the spring of 1869 began, minor repairs were made to the lower boat slip, and one entire section fifty-six feet long was renovated.

The essential fog signal called for further attention. A fog signal had been in use on Thachers for nine years. One of great power had now been set up and was considered so important — in view of the vast number of vessels dependent upon this light station and fog signal day and night — that inspectors recommended that a duplicate fog signal be kept there at all times, "so that in case one gets out of order the other will be in readiness for sounding its blast."

Officials followed through on the recommendations, and as a result the steam fog signal and its duplicate were in place by 1871. (A 12- by

14-foot enginehouse with 12-foot posts was built for the hot-air engine signal, and a 32-inch engine and a 15-foot trumpet were set up as the fog signal for the station.)

Then, while the repairs to the old buildings went on and on, and while the stoneworkers hammered away at pointing up the stonework of the ten-year-old towers, the Cape Ann twins—Ann's Eyes—reached their 100-year milestone.

Five lightkeepers and their families lived on the island now, to tend the fog signals and the twin lights, with only two houses for all of them to live in. The overcrowding caused some friction, and it was decided to build some extra rooms for the principal keeper, then Michael Dundon (1871-72), and his growing family. Congress approved an appropriation for the additional rooms, and four more rooms were soon finished in the attic to be used for sleeping accommodations.

Each change of lightkeepers brought new ideas for repairs and renovations to meet the personal needs of the newcomers. Most keepers now had their families with them, and with the two towers and lights to tend at this station, as well as the obligation to accommodate overnight any workmen, inspectors, or other visitors who might be detained by rough seas, the extra rooms were needed.

In addition to the four rooms, material was landed for a new boat slip during Dundon's period of service. The fog signal house was moved thirty feet to the south, reduced six feet in height, and set on a stone foundation with cement floors. Here the duplicate fog system was placed, and the cost of this was paid for from the "general appropriations for fog signals."

## Stormy Weather and the Storm Signal Station

While the 1870s were a period of changes on the island, they were also a time of unprecedented stormy weather. In April 1874 the schooner *General Kibon* was wrecked on the Londoner; two years later a November storm blew the schooner *Medford* off course, and it also struck the Londoner; and in 1876 a storm on June 15 sent the steam-screw freighter *Leopard* onto the northeast end of the Londoner. When this storm cleared, word got around Cape Ann that the *Leopard* carried a cargo of 800 tons of coal, and Cape Anners lost no time in helping to "salvage" the valuable cargo. By the Fourth of July, thrifty Cape Anners had carried off 500 tons of coal for their winter fuel supply!

By 1876 a new storm signal station had been set up to connect the island to the mainland by means of a submarine cable carrying telegraph wires. When a violent storm again struck the island, six months after the *Leopard*

Early photo of the north lighthouse and dwelling.

grounded on the Londoner, the new system, by means of its telegraph warnings, helped to prevent the loss of even a single vessel within a forty-mile radius of Thachers.

This storm signal system, while invaluable in storms, was nevertheless set up primarily for purposes of defense. Following the Spanish-American War the rumor spread that the signal station was about to be dismantled, a government decision for the sake of economy.

Once again indignant Cape Anners joined the keepers to protest with vehemence the removal of a single aid to navigation. Nevertheless, in spite of all protests, the government's plans for an auction proceeded. In a short time all signal equipment had been sold off — submarine cable, wires, poles, and flag — and the island settled back to the use of its own fog signal whistle. This change back to their own signal meant more work for the keepers, for now, without the aid of the cable system to back it up in emergencies, the fog signal must be kept in top working order at all times. Once again it was necessary, too, to repair the lanterns in both towers and to refit them with new dome ventilators and linings.

At this same time (1881), water pipes were repaired along with oil tanks, and a portion of the boat slip was rebuilt. The two covered ways to the towers, and the woodshed called for shingling and minor repairs as well, and a most important addition to the island — a one-and-a-half-story dwelling — was erected near the brick house by the south tower.

The south lighthouse with the fog signal, built about 1860.

## Addison Franklin Tarr—The Longest Service

The lighthouse keeper then on duty for the above-mentioned repairs was Addison Franklin Tarr. In 1882 Tarr set to work almost immediately to paint the workrooms and the dwellings of the first and fourth assistants and to repair the boat winch.

The Tarr family had one small daughter who would soon be of school age. Keeper Tarr was determined to see that Mary Gilbert Tarr would attend first grade on the mainland despite transportation problems. He solved the problem in his own way. Each morning he would lash Mary to the boat for safety, then row her to Loblolly Cove, the nearest point on the mainland. From there he walked with her to the Cove Hill Primary School, two miles distant, where he left her for the day. Late in the afternoon he returned by boat, walked the two miles again, and retrieved his small daughter for the return trip to Thachers.

The Tarr family, including a son, lived on Thachers for thirty years, a period marked by three dramatic events relating to the island. In May 1884 the Atlantic Cable was laid by Thachers door and landed at Pebble Beach, within sight of the island. While the *S.S. Faraday* lay at anchor off the island and prepared to link Europe and America with cable communications, the handful of watchers on the island were awed by this feat, as they themselves had no telephone link with the mainland.

The following summer a second incident — an electrical storm of unusual intensity — struck one of the covered ways and set it afire. As a result of this damage, extensive repairs were made, which were followed by the installation of lightning conductors on both towers as well as on the dwellings. While the repairs were in progress, an order was placed for a twenty-two-foot-long rubber hose to be ready for another fire.

## The Sandy Bay Breakwater

The third activity connected with the island was even more dramatic than the other two. Talk had already begun, and surveys, too, concerning the new breakwater to be built in Sandy Bay.

The breakwater was to be a project of national importance, and endless rhetoric was already being offered in its favor. The great dangers to navigation near Thachers had diminished but little. A recent count of vessels revealed that an astonishing 70,000 ships sailed by Thachers annually (nearly 200 per day). The same survey showed that in the eight preceding years as many as 98 ships had been total losses and that 378 more had been partial losses. Altogether, with their cargoes, the losses amounted to many millions of dollars. Such a breakwater, if built, would shape Sandy Bay Harbor into a harbor of safety second to none in the country.

Shipping interests — private, commercial, and maritime — willingly signed petitions to speed up the project. Not to be overlooked were the interests of naval officers who inspected the area and endorsed it as providing a haven for the naval fleet if necessary.

The government, petitioners pointed out, had long ago recognized the dangers here and had built six lighthouses within a few miles, two of the brightest being on nearby Thachers. In addition to the lighthouses, for twenty-five years the Massachusetts Humane Society had felt the area treacherous enough for it to establish its own lifesaving stations here and equip them with boats and lifesaving apparatus.

In short, instead of these 1,600 acres of water being a place to fear, a breakwater would serve to make them a "harbor of refuge." The advantages were numerous and were publicly proclaimed:

1. *There would be ease of access by all vessels of any size.*
2. *There would be no bars, obstructions, or intricate channels.*
3. *The harbor would always be free of ice.*
4. *It would provide excellent holding ground.*
5. *Its size — 1,600 acres of deep water (14 to 60 feet) — would prevent overcrowding.*

"There is no harbor on the Atlantic coast," proponents said, "with more advantages than this." And after an official inspection of the area, a government official announced: "The work is a public necessity."

Another report cited this to be an area of heavy seas with dangerous winds blowing from the northeast. Though the flat ledges of Avery's, Dry and Little Salvages, and Flat Ground offered some protection from the winds, these areas were insufficient for safe anchorage. "Figuring four vessels to the acre," this report stated, "these 1600 acres provide safe anchorage for fifty-five hundred ships."

The report concluded with the opinion held by most of those who inspected the area: "The construction of this breakwater as planned would render Sandy Bay one of the most magnificent harbors in the world."

The cost of this mammoth project was set at $5 million, and the work began on November 1, 1885. This time there was no question of using anything but Rockport granite, and the stone sloop *Screamer* dumped the first load of granite from the Rockport Granite Company. Soon after noon of a November day, the first stone dropped from a sling while hundreds of watchers cheered.

The work and the watching went on for years. As the end of the century neared, 1 million tons of stone had been laid, matched by a cost of $1 million spent. By 1900, nearly two decades after the work had begun, 4,000 feet of stone had been laid—not quite half of the original estimate of 9,000 feet and only one-sixth of the original estimate of the amount of stone that would be laid during that time period. The congressional appropriation for 1902 was a meager $200,000, but supporters were confident that, with the expected approval of the United States Board of Engineers, more funds would be forthcoming in a short time.

Cost of the first batch of stone was 58.3 cents per ton. The second contract, with the Rockport Granite Company, rose to 71 cents per ton. Unless weather interfered, the sloop *Screamer* dumped every day except Sunday, but when a new Congress looked upon this expensive project with alarm, the optimism of finishing it began to fade.

While efforts to interest politicians continued, year after year went by with no sign of the $8 million it was now estimated would be needed to finish the work. At last, no more funds were forthcoming from Washington. The millions of tons of granite, borne from land to sea day after day, became more of a hazard to ships than a hoped-for "Harbor of Refuge." In a short time, the storms that buffeted Thachers Island were pounding away at that great useless mass of stone that had been dumped into Sandy Bay.

# 1893-1902

OR YEARS the building of the breakwater had gone on in Thachers Island's backyard, directly under Ann's watchful eyes, while the political maneuvering was never lost to those living there. To them the ups and downs of congressional decisions were stories as old as the twin lights. Although much of the activity around the new breakwater was out of sight of the island, except from the top of the towers, for years observers watched the hundreds of ships and the thousands of spectators as they followed the progress of the stonework.

On Thachers Island, keepers went on in their daily rounds of keeping the lights and doing needed repairs. Attention of certain government officials centered on the needs and comforts of those living on the island. While routine repairs of dwellings, lights, and towers went on, the addition of 400 feet of drains improved sanitary conditions.

In addition to those requirements and repairs, some major changes were about to take place in 1895. First of all, workmen excavated a cellar under the brick house and built a porch over the back door to protect the entrance from stormy weather.

In this same year, 1895, the cistern in the fog signal house called for major repairs. Then a hoisting engine was purchased in anticipation of future needs at the signal house. In 1896 this hoisting engine was put to use to facilitate the landing of supplies, always a difficult process. Before the engine could be used, however, it was necessary to move the railroad, built some years before, to a new site more adaptable to the new engine. When all was in place, in 1897 the railroad was extended and a car was provided to carry the coal and other supplies for the signal house as well as for the tenants.

By 1900 the railroad was extended even farther, beyond the boat ramp all the way to the north dwelling — a distance of 500 feet — and a turntable was added. Also about this time, an excavation provided water storage, and carpenters built a wooden cover to prevent water pollution. All these were major improvements, but there were more to come.

## Conditions Improve on Thachers

Ever since the lighthouse board had taken over from the fifth auditor, living conditions had improved on the island. Now written instructions were sent out to keepers with details concerning operation of the lights and directions for maintaining them. After all, the lights and their upkeep must always be the first duty of the lightkeepers.

Increasingly, the repair work on the dwelling houses and towers was carried out by work crews provided by the lighthouse board, thus freeing the lightkeepers for general maintenance, such as cleaning the lights and filling oil containers. Now, the regular inspection program, organized some forty years earlier, set very high standards of performance, and in fact inspectors were intolerant of neglect of duty.

Although the keepers were not "professionals," they learned to fulfill their duties with great ability and thus provided the country with a group of trained, hardworking men and women who provided the best in aids to navigation.

In efforts of the lighthouse board to improve the image of lighthouse keepers, so tarnished by all the political patronage of the past, one new step was to replace the "hit-or-miss" clothing with uniforms. Both fatigues and dress uniforms were introduced in 1884 as standard apparel for lighthouse keepers. The dress uniform consisted of coat, vest, trousers, and cap all of an indigo-blue jersey, the coat a double-breasted style with five brass buttons in each row, each button embossed with the imprint of a lighthouse. A similar button adorned the front of the cap.

Within a year, all 1,600 lighthouse keepers then in service throughout the country were decked out in blue uniforms, resplendent with their double rows of brass buttons. If the uniforms did little to raise their morale, they must certainly have helped their clothing expenses, for the lightkeepers' pay was never more than barely adequate.

With the meager salaries, however, opportunities often arose for the keepers to augment their earnings by other means. Among these opportunities were the calls for port pilots and the constant need of repair work on the island.

In the 1800s salaries of lightkeepers had been set at $200 to $250 per year, but by mid-century they had risen to between $400 and $600. Assistants received about half this amount. Congress, in its attempts to raise the lightkeepers' morale, set the average pay in 1850 at $600 per year, where it remained until well into the 1900s.

(Eventually, on June 20, 1918, Congress passed a retirement act for the lighthouse keepers. This law permitted retirement at age sixty-five with thirty years of service, with compulsory retirement set at age seventy, at an income of three-fourths of the annual salary.)

## Some Acts of Heroism

Toward the end of the century, Addison Franklin Tarr was still the principal lightkeeper, and he must have contributed hundreds of hours to maintaining these high standards, for he remained on Thachers for thirty years!

During Tarr's tenure one of his assistants was twenty-five-year-old Albert L. Whitten. Whitten was married and his first child, Bertha (later Bertha Whitten Whitaker), was born on Thachers in 1891. When Bertha was two years old, on August 24, 1893, Whitten and another assistant, E. C. Hadley, risked their lives to save the four-man crew of the *Lottie B.*, a schooner from St. John, New Brunswick, that had struck the Londoner and came ashore on Thachers.

The *Lottie B.* had struck in a fog at 4:00 A.M., had later floated free of the ledge, and had anchored to await assistance. Meanwhile, the wind increased, endangering the crewmen, the ship, and its cargo of lumber. By 10:00 A.M. the tugboat *Cornelia* and the Massachusetts Humane Society's boat had arrived on scene, but it was too late to be of help. The *Lottie B.* had dragged her anchor, drifted onto the rocks at Thachers Island, and crashed to pieces, her cargo of lumber drifting away while Whitten and Hadley had already made their heroic rescue of the crew. Life jackets and self-bailing boats were as yet unheard of, and Whitten (and presumably Hadley) was awarded the Massachusetts Humane Society's gold plaque for heroism.

Bertha Whitten was seven years old when the famous *City of Portland* went down in a November storm (1898). On that stormy night, Albert stood watch in the north tower at Thachers. As he peered into the storm from the lens room of the tower, the north light flashed on a tossing steamship with its side wheel missing. Few believed Whitten's story that he had seen the doomed *S.S. Portland* before it went down, but later stories proved that it was quite probably true. An unidentified fisherman said that he, too, had seen the *Portland* that night, just off the Londoner, had sideswiped it with his own vessel, and had possibly damaged its side wheel!

On the mainland, the Mills family added confirmation to the story. Edith Mills recalls that as a small girl she and her family heard the mournful distress signals of a vessel, and later on her mother told her she had no doubt it was the sound of the *Portland*'s whistle as it went close by the Londoner and Thachers.

In 1899, when Bertha was eight years old, Albert went to the aid of yet another British vessel , and for this heroic rescue, he received the gift of a gold watch from British royalty.

One day, after the wreck and rescue of this vessel, Whitten stood on a rock near the water line at Thachers looking off toward the remains of the wrecked British ship. As he stood there, a wave washed in and swept over his feet, depositing a china serving plate near enough for him to scoop it out of the waves unscarred. This platter has become a cherished possession of his grandchildren, Harold and Sylvia Whitaker, the present lightkeepers. Whitten served on Thachers for nearly ten years before being transferred to Boston.

Tragedies on the island were almost as constant as repairs. While Addison Tarr was the lightkeeper, and Whitten still an assistant, John Farley, another assistant, lost his life off the boat slip. An October storm sent heavy seas running to the island, and when John Farley tried to land at the station landing slip, he lost his footing and fell into the churning water.

Harold Whitaker displays the serving platter rescued from the surf by his grandfather, Lightkeeper Albert Whitten.

Unidentified trio strikes a pose at the south light on July 28, 1896. The lightkeepers at that time were James Allison, E. C. Hadley, Frank Hall, and Albert Whitten.

In spite of the accidents and shipwrecks that at times seemed so frequent as to be almost commonplace, the very location of the island brought curious pleasure seekers as it had in Thoreau's day.

Excursions were organized on the mainland, to sail around the island, for both relaxing cruises and for whale watching (a "new" entertainment at the present time). Often a boat rode at anchor while its passengers tried to figure out the distance the twin sentinels sent their beams. Or, on occasion, when tides and winds favored them, they took a small dory to go ashore and climb the towers for the spectacular view. Some even risked going outside on the railed decks to view the endless seascapes. This was probably the best place of all for the mainlander to understand the ongoing work of the island — the saving of lives and ships.

## Innovation — A Telephone Line

Along with the pleasure seekers, the new century brought innovation to the island — electricity — and exciting was the day when a telephone line connected the towers to the houses, as well as to the mainland, by means of underwater cable (1902). In no time at all, electric clocks replaced the engines that operated boiler valves. These engines, incidentally, were not discarded. They were eventually adapted to hauling coal from the landing to the fog signal house, and then beaverlike, workmen built an earth-and-rock dam for the fog signal water supply (1903).

Although electricity was a great forward step for the lighthouse service, there was talk of another complete reorganization of the lighthouse board. The old, nine-man board had fulfilled its important work of getting the lighthouse service on its feet, but by now it had become a cumbersome and outdated head of the service. As all changes on the island were, however, this change was slow in coming.

Addison Franklin Tarr, who served the longest period of any lightkeeper on Thachers, was still there in the first decade of the new century. One of his assistants was now William Reed, keeper of the north tower. The two men had become increasingly involved with the changes in reorganization being talked about, but their more immediate concern was how to get their children to school while they lived on the island.

## 1902-1908

*I*N THE FIRST DECADE of the twentieth century there were so many children of preschool age on Thachers that the young parents voiced concern about how to get them all to school on the mainland, in a rowboat, when they reached school age.

One of the parents, William M. Reed, was then assistant keeper of the north light, having moved with his wife and two small daughters to Thachers from Race Point, off Provincetown, Cape Cod. The two girls, Alice and Louise, were mere toddlers, and their mother disliked the island life, always fearing for the safety of the children and her husband, too. Whenever he went ashore, she stood on the boat ramp and watched his boat out of sight, catching her breath each time the dory dipped into a wave, then sighing with relief when the boat reappeared. For the Reeds, however, there were pleasures as well as anxieties.

The transfer from Race Point had come on April 20, 1904, and it was soon time to pick the abundance of wild strawberries that grew on the island. The berries were so plentiful that, after pickers had eaten their fill, there were always berries left over for making jam. Fish, too, were plentiful, and there were so many lobsters that the family kept a special rock by the front steps at all times, called the "lobster rock," for cracking the shells.

When the once-a-month payday arrived, the Reed family went ashore by dory, to Loblolly Cove, as had long been the custom for the lightkeepers of Thachers. Although the monthly supplies were ordered in advance from E. E. Gray, a Boston supplier, the family had to walk three miles to the

Rockport railroad station for the supplies. The Reeds made light of what could have been a formidable problem of transporting groceries and two small children this distance. In the bushes, at Loblolly, they concealed a Good Will Soap Cart (obtained from saving coupons from Good Will Soap), and this cart made a fine conveyance for both children and supplies. On their return, William Reed again hid the wagon in the bushes, then loaded children and supplies into the dory for the return trip to Thachers.

The Reed family lived on the island for eighteen months but then moved to the mainland where the girls were able to go to school. For other island families, however, the problem of school for the children remained. Henry C. Towle, assistant keeper of the south light, had a daughter, Helen, who was about the same age as Alice and Louise Reed. (Helen is now a retired schoolteacher living in Lynn, Massachusetts.) Asa Josselyn, an assistant keeper, had a son, Asa, and assistant keeper George Kezer and his wife, Elizabeth, had a son, Thatcher Warren Kezer, born on Thachers in September 1901. Thatcher Warren Kezer, now past eighty years of age, often tells the story of his birth on the island. He relates that his father rowed his dory to the mainland for a doctor to assist in the birth, but Thatcher arrived before the doctor. Thatcher says, "I was down at the boat ramp to wave to my father when he returned from the mainland with the doctor!" Thatcher's independent spirit emerges as he spells his name with the extra t.

## More Politics Stir the Island

As early as February 1903 island parents began to voice publicly their concern over the education of their children, and politics inevitably stirred the island once more. Although some were not yet of school age, there were, from time to time, as many as eleven children to be considered.

In 1903 the lighthouse keepers of Thachers (and Straitsmouth) petitioned the courts to compel the town of Rockport and its school committee to provide a schoolhouse for the children living on these two islands, the petition to include fuel and other necessities for their comfort.

That year there were seven children on Thachers and one on Straitsmouth, and the lighthouse keepers contended that the town should either build a schoolhouse on the island (Thachers) or provide suitable transportation for the children.

The court returned the opinion that the town had already fulfilled its duty by providing schools for children on the mainland and was under no obligation to provide for the few on the island simply because it lies

The south tower from the north.

within the jurisdiction of the town. It stated that "The town may appropriate money for conveying these children to school but it is under no obligation to do so, nor if it does, is the school committee obligated to act." The court did, however, concede that "access from these islands to the mainland is always inconvenient and at certain seasons of the year is impossible."

To the great disappointment of all the island families, the petition was dismissed, and no school was ever built on Thachers. Still, in spite of the difficulties, the parents were determined to find a way to educate their children, and the teaching went on in all sorts of ways.

At this point, with a minimum of seven children on the island, the state agreed to pay for a teacher to live there. During those years — 1900-1908 — James T. Allison, an assistant to Tarr, lived with his family in the brick house at south tower. The Allisons had three children of school age, and they agreed to provide board and room for the new teacher. The arrangement was apparently short-lived, however, for the teacher fell in love with Ed Tarr, son of the principal lightkeeper. Ed Tarr was also one of his father's assistants, and when he was transferred to Boston the teacher went along with him. Their departure closed the classroom on Thachers, while parents and even grandparents helped with the teaching.

To this day, clear evidence remains of this brief venture in education. In one of the third-floor rooms of the brick dwelling, screw marks reveal where school desks at one time were attached to the floor for the makeshift classroom.

At this time, also, the government allowed one dollar a day per child for room and board ashore, and Mrs. Ben Dobson fulfilled these needs.

On Fridays the children were excused from school early in order for them to get home to the island before dark. It was their custom to walk the length of South Street to Loblolly Cove where, by prearranged plan, they paced back and forth between two poles set in the rocks. This was the signal to the island for someone to come ashore for them. When the seas were too rough for a boat to leave the island, however, the children returned to the Dobson household for the weekend.

"At that age," related Nellie Howard Jones, "we had not learned to judge ocean conditions, and often we remained ashore for weeks at a time."

At other times the problem was reversed, and a boat taking them ashore from the island would find waves breaking across the cove, making it impossible to land. Then they had to return to the island until the weather cleared.

Eventually, outboard motors came into use, and these could land at the Coast Guard Station closer to town. Later still, they were able to land at the harbor in town.

When Helen Towle was old enough to attend first grade, her father had to repeat the pattern that Addison Tarr had established for his small daughter, Mary. Keeper Towle tucked Helen snugly into the dory and rowed her to Loblolly Cove each morning, walked the two miles with her to the primary school, then returned for her in the afternoon to row her back to the island. She was nevertheless a child of privilege with one special advantage to compensate for the shortcomings of her island education. Her grandmother was often there to teach her some of the lessons the island had to offer.

Helen never forgot one of the great lessons of life taught by her grandmother—how to overcome fear. Thunderstorms were always fearsome displays around Thachers, severe and frightening enough to terrify adults as well as children.

When lightning pierced the storm clouds and sank into the ocean, and while surf churned about the rocks that hemmed them in, Helen's grandmother knew what to do to calm these fears. While the sound of the thunder rivaled that of the roaring surf, Grandmother drew Helen close as they sat on the porch to watch the storm. Then she began to explain the change of temperatures in words six-year-old Helen could understand.

"Air that is near the water is cooler than air higher up," she began. "The cooler air pushes up the warmer air and makes those fluffy white clouds. When the clouds get darker, the lightning flashes through them like an electric spark. When the cold air and the warm air meet, they crash and make thunder. Thunder," she concluded, "is just a loud noise."

Helen listened and watched as her grandmother finished her story. "Thunderstorms are enjoyed by most people on a hot day, for they cool us off. Then the rain makes the trees and flowers fresh and green again."

Helen's father, too, found occasion to teach his small daughter yet another lesson in coping with fear. At this time, snakes were numerous on the island, and a legend had resulted from them and was often repeated. Many years before one of the lightkeepers, the story went, had quarreled with his wife, went ashore, and brought back some snakes "to get back at her." The snakes multiplied, and they were a nuisance to families on the island for years, until the lightkeepers made an attempt to rid the island of them.

Henry Towle often took Helen snake hunting about the island. As they searched in the underbrush and around the rocks, Henry taught his daughter how to handle the snakes and at the same time to understand them and not to fear them.

## The North Atlantic Fleet

Along with lessons of nature on the island, there were important off-island lessons as well. In the years 1904 and 1905 the North Atlantic Fleet of the U. S. Navy often anchored in the harbor off Rockport near the unfinished breakwater, and within sight of lightkeeper Tarr and his assistants.

The admiral of the naval fleet, Bob Evans, made friends with many on the mainland as well. His friends included Charles Frederick Mills whose son, Charles Edward Mills, was then a high school student (graduating in 1905). The son, Charles (now living in a California rest home and age ninety-two), recalls the frequent visits of Admiral Evans, who came to chat with his father on the spacious porch of their South Street home. While the two men watched the tennis players on a nearby court, they talked of the fleet baseball teams and the friendly rivalry of each vessel in the fleet. The ball teams had asked permission of Rockport selectmen to play baseball on the town ball fields on Sundays when they had leave, but the board of selectmen had refused to grant them permission. "No baseball on Sunday! Not even the United States Navy."

Admiral Evans was not a man to accept defeat unchallenged. In a short time he had a baseball diamond constructed on Thachers Island. The island, under the jurisdiction of the United States government, provided a playing field for the baseball teams without breaking Rockport's strict Sunday blue laws.

At this time (according to Charles Mills and his daughter, Alice Mills Grey), Frank Haskell operated a roomy open dory, "like a whaleboat," with oars, engine, and no cabin. With this boat he ferried passengers from Loblolly Cove to Thachers for the baseball games and for family picnics. The boat held eight to ten people, and Haskell often made several trips in a day. When not engaged in this ferry service, Frank Haskell tended to his lobster pots.

Sometimes Chester and Fred Gott performed this same service from Town Wharf, but even with the games and the pleasure trips to the island, the routine work of keeping the lights in order went on as usual. Yet, in spite of the immeasurable value of the lights, vessel after vessel still ran afoul of the treacherous rocks off Thachers.

In 1908 the *Nodoc*, on almost the last day of the year—December 29—had to be abandoned off Cape Ann. Now, although the lighthouse service was working and performing heroic service to stranded vessels, there was increasing talk of change in the old service organization.

# 1908-1919

*T*HE YEAR 1910 was a memorable one in the lighthouse service. As mentioned earlier, the old nine-man board had served its time and was now considered out of date. Organized in 1852 — fifty-eight years earlier — there was no longer a need for so many men to manage the service. Although still under the Department of Commerce, it was now felt that one man could do the work of the former nine-man board.

Already uniforms were being worn, salaries had been raised slightly, and that year saw the beginning of "career men" in the lighthouse service.

Eugene Norman Larsen and John Edwin Herbert Cook were the two earliest career men to receive appointments to Thachers. Larsen was a Norwegian, born in Oslo in 1879. He married a Norwegian girl, Edvardine Reinertsen, but soon immigrated to the United States, where he changed his Norwegian name of Eugen Hjalman Larsen to the more American version of Eugene Norman Larsen. Their first child, Eugene Ernest, was five years old when the family moved from Minot's Light Station in 1911, where Eugene had first served.

In May 1912 their second child joined the family on Thachers Island and was christened Alice Thacher. The family moved from the island after eighteen months, first serving at Graves Light in Boston Harbor, then Sankety Light at Nantucket, where Eugene served until his retirement in 1944. Meanwhile, after Alice Thacher, the family had five more daughters. Maron Anton's Norwegian name became the French Marie Antoinette, but by the time the next four daughters were born Americanization was complete, and the girls received the very American names of Thelma Anne, Ethel Alma, Helen Edith, and Evelyn Doris.

Eugene Larsen served as first assistant to the aging Addison Tarr at a salary of $540 per year.

## John Edwin Herbert Cook

John Cook assumed his post on October 1, 1911, two months after Larsen. He was appointed third assistant to Tarr, with Thomas J. Creed serving as second assistant.

John Cook had been frail as a child, and like several of his predecessors on the island, he remained in rather precarious health. Also like his predecessors, he was a war veteran — of the Spanish-American War — and while stationed at Lexington, Kentucky, he had been stricken with typhoid fever. He was sent home to recuperate with a month's furlough and did not recover his health sufficiently to return to service in the Army. He was given transportation from Lexington to his home in Haverhill, Massachusetts, on a train with sleeping car accommodations and was provided an allowance of $1.50 per day for his travel expenses.

John Cook was a handsome man, although somewhat frail in appearance, with a deep cleft in his chin, brown hair, and hazel eyes. He was a constant smoker and was usually seen with either a cigar or a pipe in his mouth. When he was appointed third assistant keeper, he received a salary of $456 per year, but by 1915 he had been promoted to principal keeper, with a raise in salary to $552 per year. In spite of his medium size — he was about five feet six inches tall — and in spite of his ill health, he performed his strenuous duties well and received a commendation for assisting two fishermen on July 22, 1917, when their schooner *Commonwealth* was lost off the Cape Ann Light Station.*

John and Emma Cook had suffered a personal tragedy only a few years before they moved to Thachers. Their twin sons, born on November 13, 1904, had both died — one at the age of six months and the other at age eighteen months. The grief of the young parents had been so profound that, when a third son was born a few years later, Emma Cook could not bring herself to show her love for fear that this son, too, would be taken from her. She refused even to give this son a name until family members gave him the name of Donald.**

---

\* He had also aided in a rescue operation on January 26, 1914, when the *George W. Anderson* floundered off Thachers. He was there, though not on duty, when President Wilson's close call occurred in 1919.

\*\* Donald Cook later joined the Coast Guard and was assigned to the *Azalea*, which patrolled the coastal waters from Boston to Rockport.

A Cook family picnic on Thachers in July, 1914.

Eventually, though, Emma and John Cook were able to put their grief behind them and enjoy their remaining son. At first, in her grief, Emma had disliked the island life as much as some of the women who had preceded her had. The loneliness of the isolated island depressed her, but, like Maria Bray fifty years earlier, she was normally lighthearted and was determined to make the best of her lot. She already had a reputation as a "great" cook, and she also had a remarkably beautiful voice for singing — both ingredients to guarantee a successful party — and she began to have parties as often as her friends and relatives could get to Thachers to join them.

Emma also earned recognition as a skillful handler of boats, and an early photograph shows her in a "rowing costume" of the day — a daring divided skirt. She usually rowed standing up as the fishermen did, and she never hesitated to take off alone for the mainland in a dory.

John Cook's father sometimes visited the family on the island and was there, November 9, 1915, when he was suddenly taken ill in the afternoon and died three hours later. His death, as well as being a source of sorrow, presented an unusual problem to the John Cook family: how to transport the body back to the mainland.

Assistants on the island hoisted the usual signal of distress, an inverted American flag, hoping to attract the attention of coast guard personnel stationed at nearby Straitsmouth Island. This signal succeeded in alerting a crew who responded in a life boat, but the remaining distance from Thachers Island to the mainland, through tossing November seas, now appeared to be too great a risk to take with a small row boat. Now, in addition to the flag signal, blasts from the fog signal echoed over the water and the call for aid eventually reached the Gloucester Life Saving Station at Dolliver's Neck. With Captain King and his crew now responding, a power launch safely towed ashore the smaller boat bearing the body of Grandfather Cook. On February 1, 1918, John Cook left Thachers for a new tour of duty on Straitsmouth.

Elmo Mott replaced him on Thachers and it was Mott and his assistants who were on hand to rescue the crew of the *Mary Sears* when this boat was lost off Thachers that year.

In addition to the Cook family's emergency and the wreck of the *Mary Sears*, another peril closed in on Thachers at the end of World War I. The island was not immune to the diphtheria epidemic. George Gustafson, an assistant keeper, became ill with the dread disease and while he was violently ill his wife and six children were stricken as well. In this new emergency, it was an off-islander who came to the rescue.

Lightkeeper John Cook with his wife Emma and son Donald in 1914-1915.

The walkway and supply cart.

On that stormy October day, with the seas smashing against the coastline in fury, all efforts to get help from either Rockport or from Boston headquarters failed. Finally, in desperation, an assistant sent out an appeal to the medical staff of the Massachusetts State Guard Emergency Hospital at Salem.

The officer in charge, Major Thompson, worried about the stricken family on the island but had little hope of finding a way to reach them with medical aid. By nightfall, however, two aides volunteered to risk their lives. A "high-powered auto" sped the two men to Rockport where one of the island assistants met them with a small dory equipped with an outboard motor. Within four hours the sick family had been treated and the two heroes were back at their posts in Salem.

Elmo Mott was still in charge when the steamer tug *Kemp* struck the Londoner, but it was a far more important vessel that made the headlines in Cape Ann newspapers that year of 1919. The *S.S. America*, carrying no less a person than the President of the United States, Woodrow Wilson, narrowly escaped disaster. The ship sailed on its return voyage, from the European Peace Conference, in a fog so thick that the Thacher fog horn blew continuously. The steamship edged toward the treacherous ledges of Thachers and the Londoner, unaware of its danger, while the fog blotted out the great rock obstacles.

On Thachers, the Third Assistant, Maurice A. Babcock, stood watch that incredibly foggy night, staring out from the north tower but seeing little. Suddenly the veil of fog cleared for one brief moment revealing to Babcock the astonishing outlines of the giant steamship heading straight for the island. Stunned to silence, Babcock watched as the great ship came to a halt, shuddered like some big shaggy dog, then slowly backed away from the island—a spectre in a sea of fog. The fog signal, installed in 1871, had saved the life of the President of the United States!

The fog signal, in fact, was almost as important as the lights and had to be as carefully maintained to be ready and in operation whenever fog threatened. If a Cape Ann fog lasts for weeks, as it sometimes does, the fog signal can be heard for days on both the mainland and at sea. Imagine living on Thachers with the fog horn blowing 38,145 times! This is what happened once in more recent years (July 1959) when the fog horn blew for 211 hours without stopping. It is hard to believe, though, that it is not always the constancy of the horn that catches the ear. Those living on the island eventually get used to this sound, but more often it is only when the horn stops blowing that the listener notices its absence.

## 1919–1930

*T*HE DIPTHERIA EPIDEMIC and the plight of the Gustafson family brought to the attention of Cape Ann doctors and nurses the need for public health services. As a result of this interest, the Red Cross, after due study of the situation, recommended that Rockport hire a public health nurse. A twenty-two-year-old nurse, Leslie d'Entremont, arrived to take over this position, but Cape Anners did not accept her right away. If this new concept in health care was barely tolerated by some, however, it was readily accepted and even welcomed by those families living on Thachers. Inevitably, the young nurse would be called to assist with the delivery of a baby on the island.

Like Dr. Ezra Eames Cleaves, she kept a very irregular schedule and was on call at all hours. The October day when the two were called to Thachers was raw and blustery, and the seas were capped with white foam.

When Dr. Cleaves and Nurse d'Entremont stepped into the tossing dory, both must have had serious doubts of ever reaching the island alive. Salt water sprayed them before they were out of the harbor, and the hem of the nurse's gray cotton uniform, only four inches from the bottom of the boat, was soon soaked in the water that splashed in over the gunwales.

Leslie d'Entremont's[*] black four-in-hand tie blue wildly in the wind, and by the time the two reached Thachers the once white collar and cuffs were as limp with salt spray as was the hem of her dress. Gusts of wind whipped the blue wool cape and flashed its crimson lining, although the cape was buttoned securely at the neck with its mandarin collar. With

---

[*] Leslie d'Entremont Burgess.

a firm hand, she held on to the broad brim of the blue felt hat with its red cross sewed across the front.

The dory somehow reached the island in safety, and the baby was delivered with all the professional skill normally available for babies on the mainland. If the mainland residents failed to accept this public health service, those then living on the island must have welcomed it with warm hearts.

## A Surprise New Year's Dinner

There were five families then living on the island in the 1920s. For these families, getting supplies of food to the island — enough to last a month — required about as much effort as getting a doctor and nurse for emergencies, and perhaps even more planning. Whenever there was a period of stormy weather toward the end of the month, there was danger of running out of food. Naturally, this was the time of greatest worry, just before ordering a new supply from the mainland, but one Friday night, the last day and almost the final hour of the year, December 31, 1921, a veritable windfall came to the island.

The first assistant, William Daggett, was on duty, and he reported to the other lighthouse keepers:

*A flock of wild geese flew south about eight o'clock in the evening. As they flew into range, the light of the north tower blinded them. They crashed against the glass of the lamp chamber with a force that shattered two panes of 3 by 5 glass, three eighths of an inch thick.*

Daggett felt a draft down the tower and climbed to the lantern room to investigate. He found there a heap of feathers and one wild goose hopping about in a daze. This goose soon expired, and he discovered two more dead geese on the floor. Struggling with the weight of the three geese, each weighing about ten pounds, keeper Daggett descended the tower and called to one of his assistants, George Howard, to help in boarding up the broken windows until repairs could be made.

The following morning, January 1, 1922, the second assistant, Cantrell, discovered two more dead geese outside at the base of the tower. Five geese! A feast for the five families for their New Year's dinner!

Even more miraculous was the fact that the weather was perfectly clear and calm. Though storms often blew geese and other sea birds* off their

* Sea gulls, brant, black duck, loon, and coot, according to Henry C. Leonard in *Pigeon Cove and Vicinity.*

course, this was the first time it had happened on Thachers in fair weather.

Island families must always be prepared for stormy weather and, in fact, for emergencies of all kinds, especially the rescues. One such wreck and rescue occurred on September 2, 1921, when the *Eva Avina* sank between Thachers and the bell buoy after colliding with the S.S. *City of Rockland*. On March 26, 1925, the *Marion*, a fishing vessel, struck a submerged object and sank one-half mile off Thachers.

### Transition Years from Lighthouse Service to Coast Guard

In 1926 Simeon Orne and his wife, Geselle, moved their family of five children to the island, bringing to nine the number of children to be ferried to school each day. Simeon Orne had replaced Elmo Mott and was soon principal keeper. The Orne family remained for seven years, and meanwhile they were joined by Cecil Kelly and his wife, Florence, in 1934, along with George Seavey as second assistant. Austin Beal and Hoyt Smith followed in line as third and fourth assistants. Later on, Hubert Needham and his wife, Betty, replaced Smith. A small dog, Toby, completed the island family in the 1920s and 1930s.

Seavey and his wife, Emma, had five children, as did the Orne family, but by this time the problem of getting the children to school was partially solved. In winter weather the Seavey children boarded on the mainland with "Aunt Annie Dobson," or at times in a rented apartment with their mother, but even so, they missed a great deal of school. The government paid the board bill for the week, but the children returned to the island on weekends, and in fair weather they were boated to Loblolly Cove in the same way Mary Tarr had been rowed to school some fifty years earlier and Helen Towle some thirty years before.

Now there were five families on Thachers most of the time. They kept cows, sheep, chickens, and pigs to help out with the food supply, and the animals were always a source of entertainment as well as chores for the children.

One day Cora Seavey had a friend visiting from the mainland and, like all teenagers, the two girls wandered about the island seeking excitement. That day they found more thrills than they expected. When an ornery cow kicked at the young visitor, she lost her balance and fell into the pigpen. The terrified girl managed to climb through an open window of the pigpen. With the pigs oinking in wild confusion behind her, she escaped over a fence, where the two girls collapsed into hysterical giggles.

For Cora's father there was a different kind of excitement, and one of his duties was one that no other keeper had the courage to perform. He volunteered to paint the trim of the twin towers! It was as risky as rescue work, for the painter was only partially protected by the wrought-iron railing that circled the tower. For added security he tied himself to the railing with a rope, and he performed this duty of painting as often as necessary throughout the eighteen years of his service.

George Seavey was the principal keeper for the lights at Thachers until his death in 1945. Austin Beal was there, experienced and ready to take over when necessary, having been keeper Seavey's assistant for fifteen years. Aiding Beal were Douglas Saunders and Harry A. Wilbur, described as "a giant of a man," six feet five inches tall. In the now modernized lighthouse service, these men must not only be machinists of considerable skill, ready to repair the lights at any moment, but they must also be able boat handlers, knowledgeable about engines and, in short, well trained in the entire routine of lighthouse keeping. Nevertheless, during this period, and long before the Seavey family left the island, the hint of new catastrophe overshadowed the routine activity of Thachers.

## 1930–1933

*R*UMORS that the Thachers Island twins were to be discontinued altogether had persisted since 1922. To Cape Anners on the mainland, the idea was as unthinkable as it was to the lighthouse keepers on the island. Ann's Eyes were lanterns that had lighted the way home for generations of Cape Ann fishermen, as well as the vessels of strangers. Ann's Eyes had flashed off their coast for longer than anyone could remember. Along with the foghorn, Ann's Eyes had warned hundreds, probably thousands, of the treacherous Londoner as well as of Avery's Ledge and Thachers, but soon after 1922 the rumor began to spread up and down the coast.

While a whole new generation of Cape Anners refused to believe that anyone in his right mind would have the audacity to extinguish even one of the twin lights, the debates went on. Now repeated were the same arguments that had been offered when the towers were built in 1860. Not only were the twins unnecessary, in the view of most government officials, but they were far too expensive to maintain.

While life on the island went on about as usual, the rumors persisted. Each light, by 1927, was gas-fed to provide 22,000 candlepower. Radio and telephone connected the island with the mainland. Each family had its own vegetable garden and raised its own poultry. Fresh fish and lobster were always within reach. Still, living on the island was all too often lonely, and the single driveway to the homes on Thachers was the sloping wet boat ramp so often made impassable by a rough sea.

With Orne in charge and Seavey as his first assistant, the Great Depression made its way to Thachers. In its WPA program, the government hired local men to help maintain the island property. Manuel E. Cardoza was one of many Cape Ann men who worked on an hourly basis to help support their families in those depression years. While such skilled workmen were hired to assist the lightkeepers, about this time a new survey of all government-owned property was undertaken to determine where cuts in expenditures could be made. Thachers, as important government property, was included in this survey.

## Survey of Thacher Island

The questionnaire sent out by government officials then stated that the property — "an entire island" — was used "solely for a lighthouse reservation." It was now estimated to contain about fifty acres, jurisdiction for which was under the Department of Commerce. The survey described the property in detail:

*One double brick dwelling*
    *6 rooms each side for keepers*
*One double wooden dwelling*
    *6 rooms each side for keepers*
*One 6 room wooden dwelling for keeper*
*Two granite towers for lights*
*One brick oil house for storage of oil for lights*
*One brick fog signal house for signal apparatus*
*Two fuel houses and supply houses for dwellings.*
*Its appraised value "of about fifty acres." Land $17,000.*
    *Improvements $155,000. Total, $172,000.*
*Remarks: "Usefulness not diminished."*
*March 18, 1930*
*George Eaton, Sup't of Lighthouses, Chelsea*

In addition to the description of the property, the survey stated that although the original acquisition of the island had cost the government little, the cost of improvements had run to $155,000 in the 140 years of government ownership. This sum averaged $1,100 per year for maintenance of the island property and assured officials that "its usefulness had never diminished."

Nevertheless, with this seemingly meager sum for maintenance, and with its usefulness constant, arguments went on throughout the 1920s and into the 1930s. "Discontinue at least one of the lights as a measure of economy," politicians urged, while other officials went so far as to say the lights were "entirely unnecessary."

The north tower, 1983.

Other twin towers had actually fallen into disuse as early as 1861 when the stone towers of Thachers were built. At that time one government official had characterized holding on to the Cape Ann twins as "entirely sentimental" and had added with some disdain, "Seamen are naturally conservative." Another authority agreed that it was "Cape Ann conservatism" that had caused construction of the second set of twins to replace the original pair.

In spite of these opinions, offered when the stone towers were built in 1860, the twins had survived for almost another seventy-five years. Underlying Cape Ann's admiration of the twins—this memorial to the Thacher family, this lifesaving station—was a centuries-old pride of ownership.

The final plans emerged as a compromise: to do away with the north light and to "modernize," that is, to strengthen by more electricity, the light in the south tower.

"The new light," officials assured the disappointed citizens of Cape Ann, "will flash with one second intervals for a period of two seconds, with its former power more than doubled—to 70,000 candle power brilliance."

The "conservative fishermen" of Cape Ann were not reassured, even when told that the light would shine a far greater distance as well—"up to nineteen miles out to sea.".

"As a result of the great power of its one light," protesters were assured, "the light will shine twice as far!"

In a short time, an official ruling brought the sad news that one light must go, and in July 1930 the lighthouse commissioner proclaimed an end to the north light.

## Changes Under Protest

The Cape Ann Light Station had undergone many changes since it was first established by the Massachusetts Bay Colony in 1773 and was taken over by the United States government in 1789. From the earliest 45-foot towers, a fixed white light had shone. Then, with the towers rebuilt to a height of 124 feet, the towers were equipped with first-order (brightest) fixed lenses and oil-wick lamps. For several years, prior to the 1930s and up to 1932, incandescent oil-vapor lamps were used, each of 22,000 candlepower.

The dim 7 candlepower of Ann's Eyes had grown brighter with age, but now one of Ann's Eyes must do the work of two. The new light in the south tower was to show five white flashes each twenty seconds, and this one light was to be a magnificent 70,000 candlepower!

In spite of the tremendous power promised by the new light, the protests against the change and the loss of one twin was long.

Said Selectman Ernie Poole, "Putting out the north light is like putting out the lights in the White House!"

Cape Ann was the last of the twin lights — there had once been seven twins and one triple — along the Atlantic coast. The distinguishing characteristics of twins had not been needed for easy recognition since the new towers had risen in 1861, but for thousands of Cape Anners tradition was equally important as keeping up with modern improvements.

Though new plans presented by the government called for the south light to change from oil to electricity, the changes came slowly, as do most government projects. It took months for officials to act on their plans.

Meanwhile, the news hovered like a storm cloud over Cape Ann, and from this storm, like storms over Thachers Island, there was no escape. While the north tower lamp remained in place, it was for emergency use only, and on February 1, 1932, the new single light gleamed in its lonely splendor from the south tower.

The new electric lights in the south tower were four 250-watt bulbs surrounded by a circular lens, the lens consisting of 174 separate pieces of glass made in Paris. Once these new lamps were installed (though it had taken two years), no effort was spared to keep them in working order.

An around-the-clock watch went on, with lights checked every four hours. A stopwatch checked the flashing to make sure that all four bulbs were burning. The lightkeepers must now make corrections whenever they found an error of 1/100 of a second! Emergency power from the island's Kohler plant (a generator) backed up failures in electricity, and if both lights failed the old kerosene lamps were still available — always clean and in a convenient place at the top of the lighthouse.

The new light was too bright for the naked eye, and a mantle of pure silk covered the lens during daylight hours. Every morning the keeper climbed the spiral stairs to cover the lens with the silk cloth, and every night he repeated the climb to remove it.

Electricity for the remaining south tower light came to the island by way of the 6000-foot submarine cable to the mainland. Though a light of greater intensity shone out to sea, for those on the mainland much of the allure of Ann's Eyes had been lost.

After awhile the disappointment faded for some but never quite disappeared. "The luminous twins," one admirer said, "hold a firm place in the hearts of all."

In the end, this replacement for Cape Ann's lost love cost just about as much with no saving realized, for the north light had to be maintained, though not lighted, for a back-up system. The south tower light kept on shining.

"Perhaps one day," another admirer said wistfully, "folks may come to have for it something like the affection in which the twins have always been held at sea and ashore."

Fifty years later, on the mainland one mile away from the island, the protest still goes on.

## 15

## 1933–1939

*E*VEN WITH the north tower light in darkness, Cape Ann's love for its twins never waned, and the single south tower light continued to reach out to those in distress. While the darkened twin cast a gloom over the mainland, the routine of island life went on about as usual.

In 1933 a storm washed away the boat slip — no new thing for this had happened twice before within a decade. Again men were sent from the mainland to repair it as they had been sent when it was first built in 1842.

Whenever such damage occurred, the families on the island prepared meals and made up beds, as required of them to accommodate repair men for overnight stays. The Seavey, Orne, and Kelly families lived there at this time, and Hubert Needham for part of the time. (Keeper Beal came to assist in 1945, then replaced Needham, and later that same year succeeded Seavey.)

In spite of the loss of the north light, and in spite of the storms severe enough to wash away the boat slip three times, the work of Thachers went on. The children growing up on the island were learning to swim, to fish, to tend children younger than themselves, and to entertain each other with ghost stories about the island.

One story often repeated by the children was the tale of a headless man. Whenever fog shut off the island from all living things, the headless wraith was said to drift about the island, searching for no one knew what.

Children learned to swim by jumping off the rocks, and they often went fishing, too, with keeper Kelly, who rowed his pea pod while the children "jigged" for mackerel or pollack. Sometimes they tunneled about to try and locate the long hidden grave of Elizabeth Avery, and sometimes they made an effort to "dig for a pot," as had Ebenezer Poole 150 years before them. There is no record of the grave except the words of Anthony Thacher; no recorded vision of a headless man; no boasting of a pot of gold on the island, but curiosity and mystery abound.

Children on the mainland, from time to time, were as curious as those living on the island. Young Francis Haskell, as a boy in the 1930s, went often to the island to visit the Kelly family. Francis and his father ferried visitors to Thachers — a distance of one mile from Loblolly Cove, where the Haskells owned land and a fleet of dories. When business lagged, or while waiting for sightseers to wander about the island, Francis roamed barefoot over the rocks and poison ivy, with little concern for the outcrop of Canada thistles of Charles Wheeler's day. With one of his father's fleet of six dories as a ferry, young Haskell charged passengers a dollar to travel the single mile. When wind and tide cooperated, he timed the trip to one hour each way. He pointed the bow of the boat toward the north tower and rowed straight for the lighthouse, until he felt the pull of the tide draw him directly southwest to the boat slip.

Transporting animals to the island was an entirely different problem. One day Haskell helped Kelly ferry a cow and a bull to Thachers, an effort that paid off with a large pitcher of fresh milk on the dinner table whenever Francis visited the Kellys. Kelly, like many keepers who preceded him, was as much a farmer as a mariner, and he was determined to get the two animals safely to the island.

With Cecil Kelly directing, and Haskell assisting, the men managed to tie two dories together by means of two-by-fours attached to a board between the boats. They then led the cow onto the board, and by gently easing in and out of the tide the two men succeeded in getting the cow ashore on Thachers without mishap. This effort brought fresh milk to the island for the children, with some left over for the pigs. Two or three quarts of milk on the table at mealtimes was customary. Pigs, incidentally, were transported to the island in burlap sacks. Although the two men had to swim the cow the final stages of the trip onto the boat slip, it was worth all the effort, they agreed, to have an ample supply of fresh milk.

When Kelly decided to add a bull to the growing number of farm animals, however, this presented an even more difficult problem. First, the men managed to tie the bull's forefeet together, then the hind feet. Then, with one man pulling from the front and the other gently pitchforking from the rear, they worked the reluctant bull into the dory, all the time fearing that he would either swamp the boat or go overboard.

Margeson painting of Thachers from Loblolly Cove shows house by north light later destroyed by fire.

The precarious trip ended without incident, and the Kelly family stayed on the island for twelve years. Said Kelly some years later, "I have watched more sunrises, more sunsets, and climbed more stairs than anyone I know!"

The Haskell fleet included at least one boat with a small motor for such ferry service as mentioned earlier, and by this time constant boat traffic circled the island. Haskell once read a keeper's log that recorded seeing 300 sailing vessels passing Thachers and Straitsmouth on a single day, not to mention smaller lobster boats and other fishing and pleasure craft.

During the depression years, Thachers Island families obtained not only their own milk but also much of their staple foods from their own acres. Each family tended a vegetable garden and canned produce for winter use. One year Kelly's wife, Florence, canned an entire carcass of slaughtered beef. Sheep not only supplied island families with food; they also provided wool for islanders and for many living on the mainland as well.

One bundle of wool, very much like the wool saved by the Cook family thirty years before, was sheared at this time and taken to Mrs.

Thachers in a 1928 storm from Eden Road.

Hilma Anderson Johnson on the mainland (1934). Mrs. Johnson, mother-in-law of Esther Johnson, then carded, spun, and dyed the wool and knit it into a handsome sweater for her son. The yarn, dyed a soft chocolate-brown, contained bright flecks of green, red, and yellow woven into the brown from odds and ends of yarn given to her by friends to be used in this way. (The spinning wheel used to spin this beautiful Thachers Island wool is now in the possession of a grandson, Donald Johnson.)

The end of the 1930s and the end of the depression years paralleled the end of another era on Thachers. It was time for yet another change.

## 16

## 1939-1967

*T*HE U. S. COAST GUARD assumed the duties and responsibilities of the lighthouse service in 1939. The changes in reorganization were slow to reach the island, however, and the career men of the lighthouse service remained to perform their work as usual.

George Seavey was the principal keeper until his death in 1945, when Austin Beal replaced him. Simeon Orne had left in 1933 when George Seavey, already an experienced keeper there for six years, replaced him. Now assisting Beal was the first assistant, Harry Wilbur, the "six-foot giant," and Douglas Saunders.

For the next thirty years, after the Coast Guard took command, they operated the south tower at Thachers, and they carried out their duties with military precision. The Bureau of Lighthouses, established in 1910, had carried on inspections that were constant and thorough, and these inspections went on with a disciplined routine. Frequently, they were unannounced.

Alice Reed Brown recalls a day when inspectors arrived without warning, so early that the Reed family had scarcely put away the breakfast dishes. One inspector whisked a white-gloved hand over the arm of a chair, scrutinized the white glove, and said to her grandmother, who was visiting on the island, "I find no dust." The immaculate housekeeper replied with some asperity, "Did you expect to?"

The same meticulous inspection went on while the Seavey and Orne families lived there, and in the 1940s yet another housewife, Nancy Lee

Gray, whose husband was in the Coast Guard, endured the same white-glove inspections.

## Fire Threatens the Island

It was while Nancy Lee Gray and her husband were stationed on Thachers that a spectacular fire threatened to engulf the entire island. The year 1948 was a year of serious fires on Cape Ann, and the fire on Thachers, though isolated and surrounded by water, was a serious one for the three young couples and a baby then stationed there.

Earlier in the year a disastrous storm, with exceptionally high tides, had knocked out electric and telephone service from the mainland, although in like emergencies the island used the standby Kohler plant to produce its own power. Now, although water surrounded the island, there was little anyone could do to contain the fire, which eventually burned "everything except the main dwellings, the whistle house, and the boat house."

Nancy Lee Gray described the fire from her vivid memory of that terrifying experience. "During World War II," she said, "Navy personnel built and manned a watch station, known as the radio shack, on the southwest side of the island. After the war, the building had fallen into disuse and to disrepair, and the spick-and-span Coast Guard decided to remove the dilapidated structure. Work crews of civilians arrived from the mainland to raze the building, but by Friday afternoon they had only partly finished their work. Wishing to speed up the work before the weekend, the men decided to burn the remaining debris. Otherwise, they must remain on the island another night or more, with the families there required to house and feed them."

The day had been calm, without a breath of wind, and the workmen decided it was perfectly safe to go ahead and set fire to the remains, which burned to the ground in a few moments, as expected. Then, leaving only a few smoldering embers in the excavation, the crews set off for the mainland.

It was not until late afternoon that the wind shifted and began to gust across the island. By five o'clock the wind had increased to a blow of fifty miles an hour, and had soon fanned the remaining live coals to flame. The wind swept over the island and spread the embers like Fourth of July sparklers, touching off dry grass and poison ivy and sending clouds of smoke toward the dwelling houses.

Men and women alike grabbed anything at hand—sticks, brooms, garden hoses—to beat at the spreading flames and to wet down the buildings. The families feared for themselves and their houses, but their greatest fear — and potentially the greatest danger of all — was that the fire would set off an explosion in the whistle house.

Such an explosion could have resulted from several sources. If the water supply from the small dam to the whistle house was cut off, the steam buildup could cause an explosion. Another danger was from dynamite stored there, as well as flares for emergency use. In addition, oil containers were stored in the whistle house.

While the fire edged closer and closer to the whistle house, firemen on the mainland had spotted the fire and, after calling the Coast Guard for transportation, were on the way to help.

The squad of six or eight men, and two coastguardsmen, departed from the Town Wharf in one small Coast Guard boat. They had loaded some 1½-inch hose aboard, along with brooms, buckets, and other equipment. The bilge was already oily from a rough sea, and one member of the squad, Brud Burbank, took one look at the oily bilge water and was immediately overcome with seasickness.

The firemen made it to the island in a very rough sea — so rough, in fact, that it was impossible for them to land on the boat ramp. They were forced to go around to the southwest end of the island (probably where Anthony Thacher landed) and make a landing on what passed for a beach area. Burbank tumbled off the boat and struggled to the shore, where he fell and lay very seasick,

Ropes were tied securely to portable pumps, which were thrown overboard and hauled to shore along with the other equipment. One house was already gone, and before the firemen could set up their equipment, the grass was burning briskly and heading straight for the squad. With no escape but the ocean behind them, they had to work fast. They laid 800 feet of hose and managed to put out the fire before it reached the two dwellings at the top of the boat ramp or the whistle house, although the fire came close enough to blacken the paint on the houses and to peel it off from their south side.

Though the fire had subsided, the sea had not, and the men were unable to leave the island safely. Thus, they were forced to stay overnight, and the next morning the seas were still so turbulent they had to depart on the seaward side. (Men of the squad in addition to Burbank were Snap Silva, Muzzie Francis, Irving Tupper, Charles Cooney, Gene Thibeault, Brad Hodgkins, and Victor Williams.)

On Thachers, one problem all too often creates another. Among the buildings that burned was a wooden cover of the well, and with the cover gone pollution rendered the drinking water unsafe. Until the cover could be rebuilt and the water tested for purity, fresh water had to be brought from the mainland.*

This inconvenience, however, was only one of many that tried the patience of Nancy Lee Gray, who caught a severe case of poison ivy from the smoke fumes of the fire. She lived on Thachers for twenty-seven months, and during this time she learned to cook meals on a coal stove. (The coal was delivered to the island by buoy tenders and was then unloaded and stored for the island families by the crews of these tenders.)

While the Grays lived there, during the night the men stood six-hour watches, from six in the evening to midnight, then from midnight to six in the morning. When they arose at six for the morning watch, they built the coal fires for the women. It was then the task of women — and it was no easy task with coal dust — to keep the paint free of soot for the white-glove inspections. Enough to keep the wives in a constant state of anxiety over their housekeeping! Spotless cleaning was made even more difficult to achieve because the paint had a dull finish and the floor coverings were battleship linoleum!

Living conditions were far from ideal for this newer generation of servicemen and their families. While in earlier days, when periods of service lasted for many years, many families of the lighthouse keepers were as close as if they were related, now, on occasion, they did not get along well. One man, who had a grating personality, was especially difficult, and all the families had trouble getting along with him. As a result, they tended to blame every problem on him whether fairly or not.

One morning Nancy Lee Gray and her husband had occasion to heap a mountain of blame on the one hapless coastguardsman. When the Grays entered the kitchen that morning, they found strings of rubbery gook all over the kitchen, even hanging in shreds from the ceiling. They traced the unsettling mess to someone who had found a golf ball on the island and had left it on the shelf of the stove to dry out. In the night the golf ball had exploded, and bits of rubber were left sticking in pieces around the kitchen. The blame for this mishap fell on the head of the "troublemaker," although it was suggested that a sea gull might well have been the original culprit in bringing the golf ball to the island in the first place.

While women were free, except for rough seas, to escape the tedium

---

* One of the most important tasks on the island is to maintain pure drinking water. Often it has to be boiled; at present it also must be chemically tested each Monday morning. This is a routine duty that must not be neglected.

of island life at any time, the men had only forty-eight hours of liberty each month. The women, however, rarely took advantage of their freedom to go to the mainland without the men. One wife, with exceptional perception, observed that some of the men who were assigned this island duty tended to become possessive and were unwilling for the women to go ashore without them. We may wonder how Maria Bray and Emma Cook would have adjusted to this situation. The twenty-four-hour togetherness was surely accepted less readily by the newer generation, and under this stress divorces were not uncommon.

At the time of the fire, the monotony of island living was relieved somewhat by the animals and the one baby. An Irish setter and a cocker spaniel frolicked happily with several cats, and occasionally sea otters sunned themselves on the rocks.

While in the decade earlier, Seavey children, along with Ornes and Beals, learned to swim off the rocks, the young couples of the 1940s were somewhat more fearful of the rocks and seldom swam. There were other fears, too. One day an enormous sea hawk, with a wing span of five feet, swooped down on the island, and thereafter those on the island were more alert and cautious of leaving either the puppies or the baby in an open area.

Supplies for the island were still purchased on the once-a-month payday, as they had been since before the 1900s. Orders for enormous sides of beef were cut in advance and ready, along with groceries, to last them for the coming month.

During one storm that kept them on the island for several days after the end of the month and that meant the end of their supplies, one family had only canned salmon left to eat. Another time, supplies of tea and coffee were exhausted, and they made do with a thinned-down chocolate pudding for a beverage. They baked their own bread and pastries but had no freezers for storage. Television had come to Thachers, and a 7½-inch television screen with a magnifier entertained them. A "jack stove" provided hot water.

Unlike their predecessors, too, these young couples of the forties seldom went fishing, and it was against Coast Guard regulations to go lobstering while on duty at Thachers, but on occasion a friendly lobsterman left fresh lobsters on the boat ramp for them.

During World War II and throughout the 1940s, families learned to accommodate to the schedule of Coast Guard personnel, relying on them and their boats for transportation to the mainland. Eleanor Orne found herself in the unique position of having grown up on the island, with her father as lighthouse keeper, and now returning as the wife of a coast-guardsman.

## Coast Guard in Full Command

As the last of the career lighthouse servicemen were being phased out, the Coast Guard now assumed complete command at Thachers. Although tours of duty were made easier by automation, they were still routine and lonely. Assignments of duty to Thachers Island, while welcomed by some, were more often accepted with all the reluctance of Albert and Mary Hale nearly 100 years before.

The general maintenance and upkeep of the south light was still the chief occupation of those on duty. For the women, there was usually a baby or two to care for, or clothing to sew for the children.

Coastguardsman Morris Gibbs and his wife lived on the island with their two daughters, who were mere toddlers, for barely one month, but in that month they experienced the most terrifying event of their young lives.

An autumn storm approached, and in the night the wind blew with such force that the front door was flung open. They got out of bed to close the door, and after fastening it securely, they went to check on the children but found their beds empty. The two little ones were nowhere to be found. Panic-stricken, the young parents dashed from room to room but found no sign of the children. Almost hysterical, they pulled open the door of a closet in the room where the children slept and found the two children sleeping soundly on the closet shelf.

This experience quickly brought to an end island living for the Gibbs family, although servicemen could, at this time, anticipate a three-day shore leave once a month.

In spite of the shortcomings of island life, most of those assigned this duty retained a sense of humor. In 1967, when coastguardsman James Faulk and his wife, Florence, made their monthly three-day trip ashore, they returned to their island home with the usual eight dozen eggs and eighteen half-gallon cartons of milk.

"Imagine," Florence said, laughing, "getting ninety-six eggs ashore on that ramp — if they survived a rough sea!"

By 1960 television was the main source of entertainment, though late shows were never popular. Workdays began at 6:30 A.M.! The one officer now in charge, with his two assistants, worked on a rotating schedule, two men at a time, with two weeks on duty and one week off.

Running up on the launching platform; the Coast Guard at the helm.

For the two men on duty the daily schedule was routine but important. They began their day fifteen minutes after sunrise by flicking off the electric switch at the base of the south tower. After doing this, they climbed to the top of the tower to tie the silk lens cover over the light. While there, they also checked the 1,000-watt bulbs to see if any had burned out.

At the end of the day, fifteen minutes before sunset, the man on duty flicked on the same switch and ascended the tower to remove the silk covering for the night.

Once a week, the two men made an extra trip up the tower to thoroughly clean the entire light apparatus. Meanwhile, advance preparations for emergencies were never overlooked. A kerosene lamp waited in the lamp deck, as it had waited for decades, in the event of loss of electricity that was provided from the mainland.

The diaphone foghorn, set off in fog by forty pounds of compressed air, had to be ready for such long-lasting fog as that of July 1959, as previously mentioned, when the foghorn blasted its warning steadily for nearly 212 hours.

In fact, so busy were these Coast Guard families that they seldom had time for sunbathing on the rocks as tourists were doing on the mainland.

USCG inspection team arriving at Thachers.

## North Light Is Sold

The north tower light, already fallen into disuse, was fast falling to decay as well, just as it had in 1775. The Coast Guard could see no further use for this once important sentinel, and they proceeded to sell the north portion of the island, including the north lighthouse, to the Federal Bureau of Sport Fisheries and Wild Life. The hopes and plans of this agency, never quite fulfilled, were to study and to care for the thousands of sea gulls now seeking refuge on the island. The plans disintegrated along with the north lighthouse, and for years nothing was done to further the protection of either sea gulls or tower.

If the north tower appeared to be a lost cause in the 1960s, there was, nevertheless, a spurt of mysterious activity about the south tower. Long after Rockport's "Harbor of Refuge" had failed of completion, Thachers Island became a refuge for a notorious lawbreaker.

## 1967

OVER A PERIOD of several weeks in the summer of 1967, a Coast Guard helicopter, off and on, flew circles around Thachers. Returning again and again, it would circle the island, and sometimes it landed on a level area cleared of rock at the top of the boat ramp. Red reflector strips outlined a helicopter pad where the helicopter landed, discharged passengers, and departed in mystery. Armed guards maintained a vigil at the landing pad and the boat ramp, while at night floodlights lit up both pad and ramp. More armed guards stood watch by the wooden dwelling house, once used by peace-loving lightkeepers and their families.

By day, if a lobsterman took his dory close to shore to recover his lobster pots, an armed guard signaled him to stay offshore.

No one answered questions to satisfy the curious, but dozens of rumors flew about the mainland. Even when suspicious Cape Anners peered through binoculars from a high point on the rocky mainland, no one guessed that Thachers was about to become a secret hideaway — a hideaway for an unwelcome guest!

Eventually, it was newspaper reporters, putting together pieces of the puzzle, who revealed in their news columns the presence of the unwanted guest on Thachers.

"This barren island," one reporter wrote, "conceals a 32-year-old prisoner named Baron — Joseph Barboza Baron — here with his wife and two-year-old child."

Helicopters, reports said, had whisked Barboza there, under guard of federal officers after he had given grand jury testimony against fellow hoodlums of the Cosa Nostra. After having a falling-out with his underworld companions, he had switched from being a key gangland figure to become a key informer. The courts charged him with being a habitual criminal and with illegal possession of guns—both adequate reasons for the grudging disapproval of Cape Anners while he remained on Thachers.

After testifying in court each day, Barboza and his family lived in reasonable safety on this tranquil island, although whatever feeling of security they may have had soon gave way to grumbles of discontent. Joe Barboza, the young hoodlum, complained about the food and living conditions, his lack of creature comforts, and the social limitations. In short, said government officials, "He raised hell!"

This newest tenant on Thachers cared nothing at all for the sea gulls that had been of such interest to the wildlife service a few years before. He cared even less for the salt tang of the seaweed that had so entranced Maria Bray 100 years earlier. He had no fear, it was said, even of those enemies who would gun him down on sight. His one wish was to be free of the island that held him prisoner in its half-mile-long, quarter-mile-wide stretch of rock. Least of all to interest him, probably, were the twin lights sending out the aid that saved lives. On Thachers, or elsewhere, life held no value for Joe, but for his captor-protectors his life had to be preserved at all costs. The costs came high.

As soon as word of his presence on the island leaked out, federal authorities feared more gangland activities. In spite of all precautions, rumors spread that "hit men were all over the place," and Barboza's testimony was still important to the courts. Government officers responsible for his safety, in order to continue his testimony, decided to go house-hunting for the notorious Joe Barboza Baron elsewhere on Cape Ann. The search for new quarters was discouraging and the house-hunting officials almost gave up, although they searched Cape Ann with all the determination of a dog sniffing a scent. At last they succeeded in renting an estate on Eastern Point, Gloucester, acceptable because this also was near a helicopter landing at a Coast Guard station.

Barboza settled into his Gloucester living quarters, which were certainly more luxurious than the stark simplicity of the accommodations provided for him on Thachers Island. Nevertheless, even here he was guarded by sixteen United States marshals day and night, while German shepherds growled fiercely if anyone approached the house.

Some said it cost at least $10,000 a month to keep Barboza under guard on the Gloucester estate. On the island it had cost somewhat less, but he had stayed on Thachers only a few months, probably about three months, when the second hiding place was found for him. Here again, no one welcomed this self-confessed gun-for-hire character.

For a few months the luxury living apparently satisfied both Barboza and the authorities. While a high fence provided the necessary privacy, a boat and helicopter service nearby gave protection to the gangster from the hit men he might have encountered on the highway.

Nevertheless, he could not escape one complaint common to all — a toothache. Though his complaint this time was genuine, the problem of getting him to a dentist proved to be as challenging as that of finding a house for him had been. A competent dentist had to be found who would be willing to accommodate his schedule to this emergency and the location of the dentist's office was most important. It had to be located away from the traffic congestion of the main street of the city to minimize chances of a hit man closing in on the patient.

At last a dentist was found who met all requirements; he was located off the main street, and there was sufficient space to station armed guards, while the dentist, with more armed guards at his elbow, eased Barboza's pain.

The prisoner was able to continue to testify in court, and his testimony led to several more arrests, while Cape Ann held this man in seclusion for about nine months. In all, seven secret indictments of would-be murderers followed his testimony, and when the case was over no one was sorry to hear that Barboza had departed.

The Justice Department* then gave him a new identity and moved him to California under the Federal Witness Protection Program.

The grim, if quiet life so briefly thrust upon him at Thachers Island and on the Gloucester estate, in no way rehabilitated Joe Barboza. Almost immediately he became involved in a murder, and it was rumored that he had tried to "muscle in" on a pornography ring. Some eight years after he left Cape Ann, he was shot down on a residential street in San Francisco, as peaceful a street, no doubt, as Thachers Island, where he had lived as an unwelcome guest.

Thachers was scarcely free of the infamous Joe Barboza when a new problem threatened to involve its entire future. Since the island was government-owned, it remained for the government to hold all options, and it now appeared that the government wanted to shed its responsibility for the famous twins.

* Under John Mitchell as United States attorney general.

## 18

## 1967-1980

*C*HACHERS was about to be abandoned for the third time in its history. Just as the island had been abandoned with the removal of James Kirkwood 200 years before, and just as rumors flew of possible abandonment in 1922, the same arguments now surfaced all over again.

"Lightkeepers here are entirely unnecessary," officials repeated, and "automation" they said, "is all this island requires."

For some, it was true that automation would end all the arguments, but for others the idea was as unthinkable as it had been generations earlier. Abandon Thachers? Abandon Ann? Leave her to an unknown fate after her 200-year vigil?

The red tape of politics was about to entangle this island once more. While the situation was different — Kirkwood had been removed for his political beliefs — politics, nevertheless, had to be considered at this time as the government prepared to withdraw its Coast Guard station from the island.

Not since the north light had been extinguished in 1932 had feelings run so deep. The unthinkable had surfaced with the loss of one of Ann's Eyes. Now, though the south light continued to shine, the government proposed leaving the island as it had been 200 years earlier — an unmanned station.

By this time, the General Services Administration had been advised to dispose of all unused property of the government, which meant, in effect, that Thachers Island must fend for itself.

If there was any way to protect this island from the government bureaucracy, or to keep the historic and beloved towers from falling victim to it, it was not immediately apparent.

Since at least one of the twins, the north tower, was now considered to be "unused property," the General Services Administration notified the town of Rockport on April 22, 1970, that it was about to begin disposal proceedings. Though the north light of Thachers, no longer in use, was included in this government program of abandonment, to Cape Anners the loss of even one twin was unacceptable. Give up one of their own children? The twins must not be separated! Again the town faced the inconceivable and decided to act.

Repairs in 1975. From left: Carrying staging to the north tower, improvised hoist to the top, and replacing a light.

## Rockport Begins Its Fight to Save Thachers

As a first step, early in 1971, a town-appointed committee urged all concerned citizens to write letters to their congressmen protesting abandonment of the lights.

Meanwhile, the committee learned that to dispose of government property certain rules must be followed. The committee then studied the rules to the letter, rules that involved so much red tape that it was to take ten years to untangle them. Time, nevertheless, was what Cape Anners needed as long as one shred of hope remained to save their twins and the island.

The Association takes over as Captain David Flanagan wishes Ned Cameron well.

The town committee now began to eliminate the five options available to it. Ironically, the first step was one of inactivity. They must sit back and wait for the General Services Administration to proceed. This agency was essentially an abandoned properties dealer for the government, and its initial role was to ask all interested government agencies to bid on the properties. If all federal agencies either rejected the offer or showed no interest, the same offer was made to the state for a possible second refusal.

As a third step, if the state showed no interest, then the chance to bid on the already deteriorating property went to neighboring communities. (At the base of the north tower at Thachers lay broken sea gulls and chunks of broken glass, to say nothing of acres of rampant poison ivy.)

At this point, as a fourth option in the government's book of rules, the property is offered to public charities. The fifth and final option, if all else fails, is to auction off the property to anyone willing to make an offer.

Each step moved along in its own time, but as the options were eliminated one by one, local officials, fearful that by some action the island might still slip out of their hands, became more determined than ever to retain custody of their "children."

Before the property could reach the auction block, Rockport and Gloucester officials decided to intervene through other — though properly

The USCG helicopter heads for the mainland.

legal — channels. They appealed to the Office of the Secretary of Transportation John Volpe, a Massachusetts man.

Secretary Volpe referred the matter to Richard Hale, then the acting director of the Massachusetts Historical Commission, to inform the commission of their concern for the future of this historic property and of the possible loss of the twins to some outside interest. At the same time, local officials sought the attention of other state politicians, and all but one responded with a promise of help.

Commissioner Hale went one step further before the property could reach the auction block, and now the project took a new turn. He promised to bring to Rockport town officials the necessary instructions to seek government funds for preservation of the property as a National Historic Landmark.

More time went by as each legal move was studied and worked out, but eventually Commissioner Hale informed Cape Ann officials that, along this new route, two options remained for them.

1. The Coast Guard could empower, that is, license the town to look after the property.

2. The community could request the government to include that part of the island, the north tower (still owned by the National Fisheries and Wildlife Organization) as a national historic shrine (or monument) under

the National Historical Preservation Act (Public Law 89-665 of the 89th Congress).

In regard to the first option, for the Coast Guard to license the town committee, there were a number of disadvantages. Among these was the most obvious cost of repairs and maintenance, which could rise substantially, over a period of time, to meet changing government standards.

Option two—to seek to have the north tower (already abandoned) registered as a historic monument—was a more attractive solution. With the north tower once listed on this register, the committee realized, federal funds would then be forthcoming to match community funds. With this decision made, however, another game with another set of rules then had to be played out, this time between the Rockport board of selectmen representing the town and Coast Guard officials representing the government. Both sides must present the property fairly, while Commissioner Hale served as advisor-intermediary in the exchange.

The spadework for listing the north tower as historically important began at once, while town officials pushed out of their minds the very thought of one of their twins falling into "alien" hands. In the end, and after months of discussions, the town succeeded in holding on to the north light—only to realize that gaining custody of this light was merely the beginning. Once listed in the National Register of Historic Places, funds must be forthcoming from both town and government.

By December 1979 the state announced that the north light had been placed on its list of historic places to be restored. Since Commissioner Hale had acted as "broker" between the Coast Guard and the town of Rockport, he now urged the Rockport officials to plan their next moves with extreme care, suggesting that the town appoint a working historical commission (as sanctioned by state law) to help move the project forward. For now, the Coast Guard was impatient to make a definite move with the property.

Up till now, Gloucester men* had joined Rockport officials in the final decision for a preliminary survey of needed repairs and costs. A first estimate for basic repairing of broken windowpanes, plaster work, and removal of dead sea gulls ran from $10,000 to $15,000. Soon after this meeting, the Gloucester men withdrew (feeling that it was essentially Rockport's decision), and in March 1980 the town of Rockport followed Hale's suggestion to appoint an official historical commission. The new

* Gloucester men first serving were Harold Dexter, John Hartford, J. Veator, and Gus Lafata. Rockport was represented by Ernie Poole, Ann Fisk, Herbert Carlson, Nicola Barletta, Harold Beaton, and Ted Tarr.

official town committee appointed in 1980 included Ned Cameron as chairman, Robert Ahonen, Raymond Parsons, Gene Lesch, Rosemary Lesch, Bruce Drohan, Frank Gray, John Lane, Robert Dixon, Phillip Bissell, William Hahn, John Bennett, and Harry Walen.

Under the leadership of Ned Cameron, this town-appointed committee undertook a general cleaning-up of debris, followed by repairs that could wait no longer. Actual restoration would have to wait until such time as a caretaker could be found to watch over the property once it was restored.

### The Coast Guard Departs from Thachers

By December 1980 the Coast Guard personnel had packed their belongings and prepared to leave the island — that is, abandon it to computer technology and to the guardianship of the town of Rockport. By now, all those concerned with the preservation of this island had agreed that this bit of history, this monument to Anthony Thacher, this island that had saved so many lives must not be allowed to die. It must never be abandoned to its wild beginning. The south light, they said, must continue to shine, with the continuing help of the Coast Guard. The historic towers must not be allowed to deteriorate further nor to fall victim to further vandalism. Though the north light was out and the south tower light was now completely automated, Thachers must still have a lighthouse keeper.

## 1980-1981

*C*HOOSING the right island keeper, the committee agreed, was crucial to the success of its efforts to preserve the island.

By this time, the committee had reorganized for the work ahead and officially become the Thachers Island Association; it was now empowered to make all decisions for preservation of the island, subject to approval of the town of Rockport.

The first matter of business for the Thachers Island Association was the selection of a lightkeeper, and the search began as soon as the committee could determine what qualifications they sought for the job.

Almost at once the committee realized that the man they sought must be unique, for the work itself had changed considerably since earlier days. Whereas, for those early keepers, tending the lights was the most important work, now light tending was out of style; the old north and south lights were "unmanned," with the Coast Guard assuming all care for the computerized lights. In short, the new keeper was to be no lightkeeper at all. While he must keep up with repairs and general maintenance, he was essentially now a "lookout man" — an extra eye for Ann. In addition to the repair work, he must also be on constant watch, not so much for distressed vessels (the Coast Guard would take care of this), but for vandalism to the property he had been hired to protect.

The salary was little more than a token payment of supplies and living quarters, but it was all the committee could afford to offer. Still, the search for a lighthouse keeper proceeded with as much careful screening of candidates as for a high-salaried executive.

Though the duties, under the new light system, were to be different in scope from those of any previous keeper, and were not too clearly defined in the minds of committeemen, the group relied on a "gut feeling" for the man they sought. Not only must their man be energetic and agreeable, the committee felt, but he must be an able boat handler, an all-around handyman, and above all, must have a spirit of adventure.

For some, it seemed an impossible choice, for in addition to those requirements, and the meager salary, the man must serve alone, something no keeper had done before. Always before, the keeper's assistants had been on hand to help relieve the monotony and the loneliness.

In spite of the unusual qualifications, or perhaps because of them, the painstaking search resulted in the selection of a man as rare in character as the twin lights themselves. Sixty-three-year-old Russell Grubb, a retired bank employee, was the first keeper chosen under the new system, and he looked upon his assignment as the committee had hoped, in the same way Maria and Alexander Bray had approached it, as an "adventure."

"The work will be a challenge," said the new keeper. "I believe a man should accept each new challenge in his lifetime and give it a good try. I'm looking forward to this experience with a great deal of anticipation."

In Russell Grubb the committee knew they had much more than a man seeking excitement. Right away they recognized in this bank employee turned island keeper at least some of the qualities they sought. What if he did not know much about repairs? Or carpentry? He could learn. What if he knew little of boat handling? There were those about Cape Ann who could teach him. As for living alone, he remained undaunted by the prospect of a cold and lonely winter. "I am sure it is not the life for all," he said. "Perhaps it takes a special kind of person. Maybe you have to be a little crazy. I intend to make it, though, through the winter."

On the day of the official transfer of this island from Coast Guard supervision to the custody of Rockport committeemen, Russell Grubb was on hand to take up residence alone on the island and to assume responsibility for this historic gift to Anthony Thacher.

The ceremony, a combined welcome to the new lightkeeper and a leave-taking of the Coast Guard, was formal on that December day in 1980. Two helicopters landed at the top of the boat ramp, on the pad once used by the underworld figure, Joseph Barboza Baron. In two trips from the mainland the first helicopter transported the entire town-appointed committee. A second helicopter took its turn to land in the narrow area with Coast Guard officials from Otis Air Force Base, who were to sign the final papers of transfer. There were a few newsmen to witness and report on the emotional exchange, cut short by a bitter winter wind.

On this week before Christmas, while the cold solitude of Thachers closed in on Russell Grubb, the last of the two helicopters soared aloft toward the mainland. Except for his dog, Bosely, and a cat, Charlie (soon renamed Thacher), he was alone on the island, in a solitude he was to find himself quite unprepared for.

As the sound of the helicopter motors faded in the distance, Russell Grubb turned his back on the mainland and headed up the path toward his new home. Never had he felt more alone than at this moment. "My island," he thought, and for a brief moment of time the island belonged to him. A sense of anticipation for this new and challenging experience swept over him, and he realized what a rare opportunity lay before him.

The telephone rang constantly for the next few days. People Russell had never met called to wish him well in this Christmas season. He felt like a celebrity on his one-man island. On the third day the sea whipped up the first of its many wild moods, and Russell watched from his second-floor bedroom window as the waves pounded and broke over the ledges.

It was time for some housekeeping, and he used this day to rearrange the living room furniture to his taste. He found the furniture well worn but comfortable enough to suit his modest needs. Then, feeling more at home, he began to consider some minor repairs and engineering duties assigned to him by the Coast Guard.

Only then, faced with repairs, did the new lightkeeper realize that in his enthusiasm for this "adventure" both he and the committee had overlooked his limitations! Not only was he unprepared for the solitude and the loneliness that were soon to overtake him, he had almost no experience as a handyman, even less as a boat handler. About all he had to offer, after all, was his inclination for a new adventure.

His first job was to weather-strip the brick house where he lived, and the duct tape helped to seal off some of the cold drafts. For now, the winter freeze closed in on Thachers as relentlessly as did the prospect of a Christmas alone on the island.

On the day before Christmas a surprise visit by three members of the Thachers Island Committee — Ned Cameron, Rosemary Lesch, and Bruce Drohan — brightened the holiday season considerably. In an open Navy skiff, they battled rough seas to deliver his Christmas mail and presents intact, though arriving in a soaking wet condition themselves.

For his Christmas dinner, he cooked one of his gifts — a smoked ham from Rosemary Lesch — serving a man-sized hamburger for Bosely while Thacher, the cat, stuffed himself on canned tuna. On Thachers Island, that Christmas Day of 1980, the temperature fell to eight degrees below zero with forty- to fifty-mile-an-hour winds.

Russell sipped at one of his Christmas presents, a bottle of Dewars Scotch whiskey and opened other presents. Though lonely, he was never really alone on that Christmas Day. His phone rang all day with calls from his family and friends. He made calls himself, to his daughter in Maine, to friends with whom he had often spent the holidays, and to that friend of all islanders — Edward Rowe Snow.

The day after Christmas the temperature on the island rose slightly, to two degrees above zero. Ice glazed the rocks; the ocean looked like a mirror; and sea smoke curled offshore. Russell eagerly awaited news of a new grandchild expected on New Year's Day.

## Winter on the Island

Russell's first winter on Thachers was a cold and lonely four months. Although in mid-January a friend, June Morris, came to join him for a time, he often wandered the island and wondered if "out here" was really for him. There were many days with nothing more to do than to watch television, read, sleep, and eat too much.

By the middle of February, both Russell and June were getting cabin fever. A pea soup fog socked them in for a week. Rain and wind beat against the windows, and the cellar flooded. They grew tired of television programs, and their supplies dwindled.

There were other problems that neither the keeper nor the committee had to solve. As had often happened in the past, the electronic foghorn* failed to function. Then, toward spring, the south light was out of order for three days. Though the emergency light system replaced the defective light temporarily, it afforded a dim and unsatisfactory beam. For these emergencies, the Coast Guard provided funds and experienced servicemen for the repairs.

## Spring Comes to Thachers

Spring crept on slow feet toward Cape Ann and Thachers Island. Russell Grubb tested his carpentry skills by building a tabletop box to hold June's books and radio. When the temperature permitted, he went outside, and with some help from a friend, he framed up a creditable henhouse. By early June the fresh green of the poison ivy flourished all over Thachers. Grass grew tall enough for mowing about the house and the helicopter

---

* The foghorn equipment sends out a strobe beam from the south tower, and a chart records how much light the fog reflects.

Seagulls on Thachers . . .

pad. Hundreds of sea gulls nested on the rock shelves, and their hen-sized eggs began to hatch. The keeper had little time to be lonely now.

The Thachers Island Committee kept him informed almost daily, either by phone or a boat trip, of their plans for the island. Along with the sea gulls, Bosely, and Thacher, a ram and an ewe, on loan from a Cape Ann farmer, joined the island family.

For several days, in mid-June, the two sheep could not be found, and a thorough search of the island revealed no sign of them. Though Grubb and the Thachers Island Committee worried about their missing "children," the animals continued to elude searchers. At last, the Coast Guard helicopter was pressed into service to make several flying trips over the island, but the two sheep remained unaccounted for until one day at dusk. Bosley began to growl while, as was their custom, dog and master stood near the boat ramp surveying Sandy Bay. First the ram appeared from the underbrush, then the ewe, then — to the astonishment of both Grubb and Bosely — a baby lamb tagged behind. After permitting themselves one brief "baa" of pride, the sheep returned to the underbrush.

Eventually, three goats, a mother and twin daughters, joined the family, and when a friend brought five hens from the mainland to live in the new henhouse, keeper Grubb said "enough." Though the hens usually pro-

. . . and a ewe and a lamb.

duced two or three eggs per day, storm and foghorn upset their peace of mind and lowered their production.

The animals grazed as happily as had the oxen centuries before them, keeping the grass well cropped without man's efforts and, to the surprise of all, poison ivy became a delicacy they munched at will.

In spite of the grazing animals, brought to the island by a boat un-officially dubbed "Noah's Ark," the once nonexistent brush grew six feet high. With little money for hired help, the committee called for volunteers to tidy up the island for its first visitors. "Workdays" were organized with the group to clear up the debris and the overgrown brush. Though goats and sheep munched the grass, they made only slight headway in the tangle of brush that grew all that first summer of 1981, as the committee's plans moved forward.

## 20

## 1981-1982

*A*LTHOUGH AN AUTOMOBILE will probably never spin its wheels up the boat ramp at Thachers, a landing barge was, in the summer of 1981, among the dream plans for the safety of future visitors. The hardworking committee never forgot for an instant that the island belonged to Cape Ann and its visitors. Committee members continued to wrestle with the often unwieldy plans for the island's future. Their dream of some kind of a landing barge loomed bright but visionary.

At the same time, keeper Grubb struggled with his own future. After six months, he still enjoyed many aspects of island life – its serenity, its natural beauty, the excitement of holding in his own hands the awesome responsibility for this unique position. Yet the upset of contractor's equipment coming to work on the installation of a septic system, combined with the prospect of another lonely winter, disturbed him.

One night, unable to sleep, he climbed to the lens rooms at the top of the south tower. His watch showed 3:00 A.M. Even the gulls were silent. The moon hung low over Cape Ann and splashed a path of shimmering gold all the way to Europe. Under the magic spell of the island, keeper Grubb was captivated anew.

All too soon, however, August brought reminders of another winter. Wild wind rattled the windows all one night, while high tides flung seaweed and smashed lobster gear over rocks and the boat ramp. A piece of plastic covering blew off the roof of the hen coop, and Russell promised himself to shingle the roof without further delay.

North tower cleanup crew members (from left): Judy Hubert, Chip Norton, Charlene Brown, and Lauri Parrot.

Questions concerning his own future mingled with the committee's plans for the island and kept his mind in turmoil. A September storm repeated the ravages of August, with the sea spray blowing to the top of the whistle house roof. Though Russell Grubb still considered it a privilege to be able to observe nature's spectacular shows from his unique theater, he avoided the issue of another winter alone on the island.

### Autumn on the Island

By September there was still no landing barge to transport visitors to the island, but the Thachers Island Committee planned a clambake on the island as a gesture of thanks for all those who had volunteered hours of labor to "houseclean" the island.

True to the island's past, a storm upset all plans for a Saturday clambake, making it impossible for the volunteer boaters to land in safety. The clambake had to be postponed until October, when clear weather favored the group on the last day they could count on for a picnic before winter weather closed in the island.

The clambake menu contained far more than clams. After a bowl of clam chowder, served hot with crackers, came the steamers, as many as

Clambake 1981 . . . above, the lobsters . . . below, the happy guests.

Clambake 1982 . . . above, the lobsters . . . below, the chowline and keeper Harold Whitaker.

one could eat, along with a choice of barbecued chicken, lobster, or steak. If this was insufficient fare for the hungriest, there was more to come; an ear of corn, cole slaw, hot rolls, home-made cookies, a slice of watermelon, and steaming coffee. All this, eaten on wooden folding tables and chairs, was flavored with vistas of ocean in all directions.

For keeper Grubb, on hand as official host for "his" island, a rare year as the first civilian keeper of Thachers Island lights drew to an end. One day, soon after the clambake, he summed up his experiences — as had other keepers before him — in a letter to the *Gloucester Daily Times*.

Meanwhile, in this miniature National Park, a few more weeks of fall rounded up the year's work program, as Chip Norton, trained in botany and forestry at the University of Maine, volunteered yet more hours in clearing footpaths and picnic areas, every inch of the more than fifty acres with unsurpassed ocean view.

"It is another world," said one committee member, and Russell Grubb agreed. "The island is a paradise for bird watchers, fishermen, botanists, and for all those who have a heart for historic sights and places."

By November a new boat winch was in place, and for the new septic system, a backhoe, a compressor, cement tanks, and fifty drums of gravel were unloaded from a barge onto the ramp at high tide.

Russell Grubb began to think of leaving while marooned for four more days by six- to eight-foot waves from a storm that swept away some of the contractor's equipment.

## To Watch and to Wait

The work of the island was changing, but still much remained the same as in the days of James Kirkwood, Sam Huston, and Joseph Sayward. Now, however, there was a new expectancy. At the end of the project's first year, it was clear to all — mainlanders as well as to Russell Grubb and the Thachers Island Association — that the island was a heritage worth preserving.

Within the year the first dream of a landing barge took shape from a wooden boat model made by Chairman Ned Cameron, and this model gave shape to the entire program as well. Ultimately, this landing barge became a reality, custom designed of aluminum for its unique work. It was christened on July 11, 1982, and shortly after was put to use carrying its first load of visitors to the island.

Rosemary Lesch, Thacher Island Committee member
christens the new craft at T Wharf on July 11, 1982.

*Today this island of the* Watch and Wait *... island of Anthony Thacher and his tragedy; island of all those who have come after him and called his island "home"; island of fishermen, farmers, artists; island of grief, of trouble, of discord; island of the strident, hoarse voice of seagull and fog horn; island of storms both physical and political; island of shipwrecks; island of life-saving light ... watches and waits for its future to unfold.*

*Though in some distant time Ann's Eyes should dim to the light of a single candle, her vision will survive the ages. For on Cape Ann, many believe that those who live near lighthouses look up more often.*

# Bibliography

A Guidebook, Along the Roads of Essex County. Boston, Junior League of Boston, 1970.

Babson, John J., History of Gloucester. Gloucester, Proctor Bros., 1860.

Babson, Roger W. and Saville, Foster, Cape Ann (A Tourist Guide). Gloucester, Cape Ann Community League, 1952.

Bentley, William, Diary. Salem, Essex Institute, October 1814.

Brayley, Arthur W., History of the Granite Industry of New England. Boston, E. L. Grimes, 1913.

Cape Ann Scientific and Literary Association, Along Old Roads of Cape Ann. Gloucester, F. S. McKenzie, 1923.

Carter, Robert, Coast of New England. Somersworth, New Hampshire, New Hampshire Publishing, 1977.

Coast Guard Academy, Library Collections. New London, Connecticut.

Copeland and Rogers, Saga of Cape Ann. Freeport, Maine, Bond Wheelwright, 1960.

Eliot, T. S., Collected Poems. New York, Harcourt, Brace and World, Inc., 1930, 1963.

Gott, Lemuel, History of Rockport. Rockport, Rockport Review Press, 1888.

Hawes, Charles B., Gloucester by Land and Sea. Boston, Little, Brown, 1921.

Hawthorne, Hildegarde, Old Seaport Towns of New England. New York, Dodd, Mead, 1916.

Holland, Francis Ross, Jr., America's Lighthouses. Brattleboro, Vermont, Stephen Greene Press, 1972.

Johnson, Esther, Papers. Rockport.

Kenny, Herbert, Cape Ann: Cape America. Philadelphia and New York, Lippincott, 1971.

Leonard, Henry C., Pigeon Cove and Vicinity. Boston, F. A. Searle, 1873.

Morison, Samuel E., Maritime History of Massachusetts. Boston, Houghton, Mifflin, 1921.

Pool, Ebenezer, Papers. Rockport Library.

Pringle, James R., History of Gloucester. Author, 1892.

Proctor, George, Fishermen's Memorial Record Book. Gloucester, Proctor Bros., 1873.

Records of Early Gloucester. Rockport Library.

Rockport Anchor. Rockport Board of Trade, 1966.

Rockport Review, Ye Headlands of Cape Ann. Rockport, Press of Rockport Review, 1902.

Salem Register. Salem Library, 1960.

Shurtleff, Nathaniel, Collections. Salem Library.

Swan, Marshall W. S., Town on Sandy Bay. Canaan, New Hampshire, Phoenix Publishing, 1980.

Swift, Charles F., History of Old Yarmouth. Portland, Maine, Atheneum Press, 1876.

Verrill, A. Hyatt, Along New England Shores. New York, G. P. Putnam, 1936.

Webber, John S., Jr., In and Around Cape Ann, Gloucester. Cape Ann Advertizer, 1885.

Young, Alexander, Chronicles of the First Planters of the Colony of Massachusetts Bay. Boston, Little, Brown, 1846.

# Lighthouse Keepers and Their Assistants

The records of lighthouse keepers and their assistants from which the following list was compiled are incomplete. The lighthouse keepers and their terms of service are shown beneath together with the names of their assistants where recorded. Thachers Island was abandoned during the Revolution and at the end of the war Stephen Choate was appointed caretaker from 1781-1784 when the lights were again lit. The last keeper, Austin Beal, appointed in 1945, retired sometime thereafter when Coast Guard personnel became responsible for the lights. The names of Davis, Cantrell, and Payne appeared in the records but were unidentifiable.

| | | | |
|---|---|---|---|
| James Kirkwood | 1771-1775 | John Cook | 1911-1913 |
| Samuel Huston | 1784-1792 | Eugene Norman Larsen | |
| Joseph Sayward | 1792-1814 | Howard W. Carter | |
| Aaron Wheeler | 1814-1834 | Thomas J. Creed | |
| Austin Wheeler | 1834-1837 | Elmo Mott | 1918-1926 |
| Charles Wheeler | 1837-1849 | George Gustafson | |
| William Hale | 1849-1853 | Maurice A. Babcock | |
| Lancelot Kelly Rowe | 1853-1855 | William Daggett | |
| James Collins Parsons | 1855-1861 | George Howard | |
| William H. Tarr | | Simeon Orne | 1919-1933 |
| James C. Parsons, Jr. | | George Seavey | |
| Benjamin Parsons, Jr. | | Austin Beal | |
| Albert Giddings Hale | 1861-1864 | Hoyt Smith | |
| Eben Abbott | | Herbert Needham | |
| Alexander Bray | 1864-1869 | Cecil Kelly | |
| Joseph Wingood | 1869-1871 | George Seavey | 1933-1945 |
| Michael Dundon | 1871-1872 | Austin Beal | 1945- |
| Albert W. Hale | 1872-1881 | Harry A. Wilbur | |
| Addison Franklin Tarr | 1881-1912 | Douglas Saunders | |
| Alfred Eisener | | | |
| E. C. Hadley | | | |
| Albert Whitten | | | |
| Frank Hall | | | |
| James Allison | | | |

# Illustrations and Credits

The illustrations in *Thachers / Island of the Twin Lights* came from many sources and the author is deeply grateful to all who were so generous with their help. In the following, each is listed chronologically in the order in which it appears with the abbreviated title followed, where known, by the photographer's or delineator's name, the source, and the page number on which the illustration appears.

Twin Lights on Thacher's Island / Painting by G. Tucker Margeson / Collection Mr. and Mrs. Story Parsons, Cover

Map of Rockport Harbor / Section of National Ocean Survey map, ii

Route of the *Watch and Wait* / Superimposed on section of USGS Rockport quadrangle map, 4

Thacher cradle / Photo by Darrel Currie, 12

Sketch of the Londoner / Courtesy USCGA Library, 16

Salary order / Courtesy USCGA Library, 19

Argand lamp / Drawing by David Battle, 26

Original stone house today / Photo by Phil Bissell, 30

Charles Wheeler's stone wall / Collection Mr. and Mrs. Story Parsons, 39

North tower before 1981 restoration / *Gloucester Daily Times* photo, 44

Joppa / Painting by Lancelot Rowe / Collection Elizabeth Day, 48

Notice to Mariners / Courtesy USCGA Library, 55

Albert Giddings Hale / Collection Virginia Eddy, 58

Mary Choate Blatchford Hale, Collection Virginia Eddy, 58

Light House for Cape Ann / Engineering drawing by Capt. A. B. Franklin / Courtesy USCGA Library, 60

The walkway today / Photo by Phil Bissell, 64

The north lighthouse / Collection George Caffrey, 68

South lighthouse and fog signal about 1860 / Collection Mr. and Mrs. Story Parsons, 69

Harold Whitaker and serving platter / Photo by Ruth Pelley, 75

Clowning at the south light, 1896 / Collection Mr. and Mrs. Story Parsons, 76

The south tower / *Gloucester Daily Times* photo, 80

Cook family picnic, 1914 / Collection Brother David Cook, 86

The Cook family, 1914-1915 / Collection Brother David Cook, 87

The walkway and supply cart / Photo by Gary Taber, 88

The north tower, 1983 / Photo by Phil Bissell, 96

Thachers from Loblolly Cove / Painting by G. Tucker Margeson / Photo collection of Mr. and Mrs. Story Parsons, 102

Thachers from Eden Road, 1928 / Photo by Story Parsons, 103

Running up on the platform / *Gloucester Daily Times* photo, 110

USCG inspection team / *Gloucester Daily Times* photo, 111

Staging to the north tower / *Gloucester Daily Times* photo, 116

Improvised hoist / *Gloucester Daily Times* photo, 117

Replacing a light / *Gloucester Daily Times* photo, 117

The Association takes over / *Gloucester Daily Times* photo, 118

The USCG helicopter leaves / *Gloucester Daily Times* photo, 119

Seagulls on Thachers / Photo by Phil Bissell, 126

Ewe and lamb / *Gloucester Daily Times* photo, 127

The cleanup crew / Photo by Rosemary Lesch, 129

Clambake 1981, the lobsters / *Gloucester Daily Times* photo, 130

Clambake 1981, the guests / *Gloucester Daily Times* photo, 130

Clambake 1982, the lobsters / Photo by Phil Bissell, 131

Clambake 1982, the chow line / Photo by Phil Bissell, 131

Clambake 1982, Harold Whitaker / Photo by Phil Bissell, 131

Christening the new landing barge / *Gloucester Daily Times* photo, 133

A window of the north tower building and a lobster buoy frame the south light / *Gloucester Daily Times* photo, 134

# Index

Abbott, Eben, 58
*Abigail*, 23
Acts of heroism, 74
Adams and Roberts, 53
Administrator, 11
Age of Ice, 2
Ahonen, Robert, 121
Aids to navigation, 15, 48, 50, 68, 73
Albany, 40, 41
Allen, Joseph, 13
Allen, Nathaniel, 13
Allerton, Isaac, 5
Alexander, B. S., 53
*Alfred*, 28
Allison, James T., 76, 81
Alterations and repairs, 32
America, 3, 26, 69, 84
*America*, 88
American Colonies, 15
*American Lighthouses*, 43
American Revolution, 19
Andrews, 5
Andrews, Mary, 20
Andrews Point, 21
Ann's Eyes, 17, 25, 67, 72, 94, 97, 98, 114, 122, 135
*Ann Maria*, 40
*Anti*, 46
Appleton, John, 13

Argand, Aimé, 25, 26
Argand lamp, 26, 27, 28, 35, 42, 45
Armed guards, 112
Army and Navy personnel, 66
Articles of agreement, 29
Atlantic coast, 2, 98
Atlantic Ocean, 1, 42, 62
Auction, 68, 119
Autumn on Thachers, 129
Avery, Elizabeth, 10, 101
Avery, John, 5, 6, 8, 11
Avery's Ledge, 71, 94
*Azalea*, 85

Babcock, Maurice A., 89
Back up system, 98
Bangor, Maine, 37
Bank employee, 123
Barber's basin, 27
Barletta, Nicola, 120
Baron, Joseph Barboza, 112, 113, 114, 123
Baseball teams, 83
Battle, David, 26
Battleship linoleum, 107
Beacon, 37, 45, 48, 49
Beal, Austin, 92, 93, 100, 104
Beaton, Harold, 120
Beehive, 42
Bell, 48, 49, 63
Bennett, John, 121
Bissell, Phillip, 121
*Bloomer*, 46
Board of Selectmen, 120
Boat house, 64
Boat ramp, 36, 37, 63, 64, 66, 68, 73, 75, 94, 100, 106, 112, 123, 126, 128, 132
Bonfires as beacons, 15
Bosely, 124, 126
Boston, 4, 15, 17, 25, 26, 31, 37, 40, 48, 49, 50, 51, 52, 53, 58, 59, 75, 78, 81, 84, 85, 88
*Boston Journal*, 53
Boston lighthouses, 21
Bray, Alexander, 59, 61, 63
Bray, Maria, 59, 61, 62, 63, 86, 108, 113

Breakwater, 2, 36, 70, 71, 72, 83
British bride, 19
British brig *Hope*, 46
British coast, 27
British royalty, 75
British rule, 15
British seaman, 20
Brown, Alice Reed, 104 (See Reed, Alice)
Brown, Charlene, 129
Bryant, Gridley James Fox, 53
Buchanan, James, 52
Burbank, Brud (Charles), 106
Bureau of Lighthouses, 104
Burgess, Leslie d'Entremont, 90

Cable, 21, 67, 69, 77, 98
California, 41, 83
Cameron, George E. (Ned), 121, 124, 132
Canada, 15, 24, 59
Canada thistles, 38
Candle, 17, 21, 27, 94, 97, 135
Cape Ann, 1, 10, 11, 13, 17, 18, 25, 27, 28,
    37, 41, 47, 48, 49, 50, 52, 55, 56, 60, 67,
    83, 88, 89, 90, 95, 97, 98, 100, 105, 112,
    114, 116, 123, 125, 126, 128, 135
Cape Ann conservatism, 97
Cape Anners, 17, 18, 34, 36, 51, 52, 56, 67,
    68, 94, 112, 117
Cape Ann history, 12
Cape Ann Light Station, 15, 17, 21, 22, 29,
    46, 66, 85, 97
Cape Canaveral, Florida, 45
Cape Cod, 5, 78
Cardoza, Manuel E., 95
Career men, 84, 104, 109
Cargo, 20, 37, 74
Carlson, Herbert, 120
Cart, 63, 79, 88
Ceded (lighthouses), 23
Champlain, Samuel D., 3
Changes under protest, 97
Charlie, 124
Chelmsford, 51, 52
Chelsea, 95
Cherished possession, 75
Chest of drawers, 19
Children, 7, 9, 10, 57, 77, 79, 81, 82, 87, 92,
    100, 118

Choate, Rufus, 34
Choate, Stephen, 21
Christened, 132, 133
Christmas, 63, 124, 125
Church, Helen Poole, 48
Cistern, 63, 65, 72
*City of Portland*, 74, 75
*City of Rockland*, 92
Civil War, 57, 59
Clambake, 129, 130, 131, 132
Clay, Clement C., 51
Cleaves, Ezra Eames, 90
Coast Guard, 15, 45, 49, 55, 82, 85, 87, 104,
    105, 106, 108, 109, 110, 111, 112, 113,
    114, 119, 120, 121, 122, 123, 124, 125, 126
Coast Guard Academy Library, 42
Coasting vessels, 20
Coffin, Peter, 21
Commerce department, 24, 84, 95
Commercial interests, 25
Commercial route, 15
Commissary General, 22
Committee of one, 21
*Commonwealth*, 85
Commonwealth of Massachusetts, 23, 24
Computerized lights, 122
Concerned citizens, 117
Concord, New Hampshire, 50, 51
Congress, 43, 45, 50, 66, 71, 74, 120
Construction of towers, 50
Controversies, 12, 29, 95
Cook, Donald, 85, 86, 87

Cook, Emma, 85, 86, 87, 108
Cook, John Edwin Herbert, 84, 85, 87, 102
Cooney, Charles, 106
*Cornelia*, 74
Cosa Nostra, 113
Cotton, John, 6
Cove Hill Primary School, 69
Covered ways, 70
Cradle, 12
Creed, Thomas, J., 85
Council of War, 12
County of Essex, 23
Court of Justice, 12
Cousin, 5, 6, 7, 8, 33

Daggett, William, 91
*Daniel Webster*, 37
Day of celebration, 17
Dearborn, Henry, 27, 29
Debts owed Avery, 11
Declaration of Independence, 23
Demonstration, 26, 27
Depression, 94, 95, 102
Derby, Richard, 13
Dewars Scotch whiskey, 125
Dexter, Harold, 120
Diphtheria, 87, 90
Divorces, 2, 108
Dixon, Robert, 121
Dobson, Annie (Mrs. Ben), 81, 92
Dolliver's Neck light station, 87

Dory, 22, 37, 57, 76, 79, 82, 83, 86, 90, 91, 101
Drohan, Bruce, 121, 124
Dundon, Michael, 63, 67
Dwelling house, 14, 29, 31, 34, 55, 63, 66, 68, 69, 72, 73, 77, 95, 105

Earth and rock dam, 77
Eastern Point, 35, 112
Eaton, George, 95
Eddystone, 24
Eden Road, 103
Electrical storms, 2, 69, 82
Electricity, 76, 98, 105
Electric clocks, 77
Ellery, William, 13
Elliot, William H., (Eliot), 5, 6
Ellsworth, Maine, 37
Engine house, 63
Epidemic, 58
Erect a lighthouse, 13
Erving, John, 13
Europe (European), 15, 28, 69, 128
European Peace Conference, 88
*Eva Avina*, 92
Evans, Bob, 83

Families, 2, 66, 92, 100, 102, 104, 105, 106, 107, 108, 110, 112, 126
Family picnics, 83, 86
*Fancy Packet*, 40, 41
*Faraday*, 69
Farley, John, 75
Faulk, Florence, 109
Faulk, James, 109
Federal Bureau of Sport Fisheries and Wildlife, 111, 119
Federal Witness Protection Program, 114
Fellow hoodlums, 112
Ferry service, 83
Fifth Auditor, 24, 42, 43, 73
Fire, 70, 105, 108
First romance, 20
Fishermen, 6, 20, 34, 35, 38, 40, 85, 86, 94
Fisher rock, 15
Fishing, 31, 32

Fisk, Ann, 120
Fixed white light, 97
Flat Ledges (Avery's), 71
Fledgling government, 24
Fog, 2, 40, 48, 54, 88, 89
Fog signal, 63, 65, 66, 67, 68, 69, 72, 77, 87, 94, 125, 135
Forefathers' Day, 16
Foundation stones, 15
Fourth of July, 67
France, 45
*Frances*, 46
Francis, Marion J., (Muzzie), 106
Franklin, W. B., 48, 60
Fresh milk, 101, 102, 109
Fresnel, Augustin, 42
Fresnel lens, 28, 42, 43, 45, 53, 54, 61, 98
Frost, D. O., 22

Gallatin, Albert, 27
Gannet rock, 15
Garrison House, 34
*Gazette*, 59
*General Kibon*, 67
General Services Administration, 114, 115, 118
*George W. Anderson*, 85
Gibbs, Morris, 109
Gloucester, 4, 13, 34, 37, 38, 40, 47, 48, 51, 56, 87, 112, 113, 118, 120
*Gloucester Daily Times*, 132
*Gloucester Telegraph and News*, 37, 54
Gold plaque, 74
Gold watch, 75
Good Will soap, 79
Gott, Chester, 83
Gott, Fred, 83
Grand Jury testimony, 113
Granite, 50, 51, 52, 53, 55, 71
Granite Industry, 50
Grapes, 37, 38
Graves light, 84
Gray, E. E., 78
Gray, Frank, 121
Gray, Nancy Lee, 105, 107
Grey, Alice Mills, 83

Grubb, Russell, 123, 124, 125, 126, 128, 129, 132
Gustafson, George, 87, 90
*Gypsee*, 58

Hadley, E. C., 74, 76
Hahn, William, 121
Hale, Albert Giddings, 57, 58, 63, 109
Hale, Albert William, 63
Hale, Mary Choate Blatchford, 57, 58, 59, 109
Hale, Richard, 119, 120
Hale, William, 40, 45, 46, 47
Hall, Frank, 76
*Hamilton*, 16
Hancock, John, 13
*Hannah and the Hatchet Gang*, 57
Harbor of Refuge, 70, 71, 111
Hartford, John, 120
Haskell, Francis, 101, 102
Haskell, Frank, 83
Haskell, Sidney, 61, 62
Haverhill, Massachusetts, 85
Headless man, 100
Helicopter, 112, 119, 123, 124, 125, 126
Henhouse, 125
Hingham, 32
Hodgkins, Bradley, 106
Holland, Francis Ross, 43
Holmes, Almoran, 53, 54
Holmes hoist (see lifting device), 54, 72

Home remedies, 61
Howard, Ethel Publicover, 48
Howard, George, 91
Hubert, Judy, 129
Humpback whales, 58
Humphrey, Noah, 32
*Huntress*, 34, 35
Huston, Samuel, 22, 23, 132

Illegal possession of guns, 113
Incandescent oil-vapor lamps, 97
Ipswich Harbor, 5
Ipswich River, 4
Island, 1, 10, 13, 18, 21, 24, 29, 31, 32, 34,
    36, 37, 38, 40, 47, 48, 53, 56, 57, 58, 59,
    62, 63, 66, 67, 73, 76, 77, 79, 86, 88, 90,
    91, 94, 99, 100, 104, 105, 108, 114, 116,
    119, 121, 123, 124, 129, 132, 135 (see
    Thachers Island)
Isle of Shoals, 5

Jack stove, 108
*James*, 4
January storm, 28
Johnson, Donald, 103
Johnson, Esther, 103
Johnson, Hilma Anderson, 103
Johnson, Walter, 51
Jones, Nellie Howard, 81

Joppa, 47, 48
Josselyn, Asa, 79
Jumper, Hannah, 57, 58
Justice Department, 114

Kelly, Cecil, 92, 100, 101, 102
Kelly, Florence, 92, 102
*Kemp*, 88
Kerosene lamps, 98, 110
Kezer, Elizabeth, 79
Kezer, George, 79
Kezer, Thatcher Warren, 79
Kirkwood, James, 17, 18, 19, 20, 29, 53, 59,
    115, 132
Knowlton, William Hale, 36, 37
Kohler plant, 98, 105

Lafata, Gus, 120
Landing barge, 128, 129, 132, 133
Landmark for Historic Preservation, 1, 2
Lane, John, 121
Lanterns, 34, 35, 36, 39, 40, 43, 45, 53, 55,
    62, 68, 94
Larsen, Alice Thacher, 84
Larsen, Ethel Alma, 85
Larsen, Eugene Ernest, 84
Larsen, Eugene Norman, 84, 85 (Larsen,
    Eugen Hjalman)
Larsen, Evelyn Doris, 85
Larsen, Helen Edith, 85
Larsen, Maron Anton, 84 (Larsen, Marie
    Antoinette)
Larsen, Thelma Anne, 85
*Lee*, 20
Lens room, 62, 74, 128
Leonard, Henry C., 91
*Leopard*, 67
Lesch, Gene, 121
Lesch, Rosemary, 121, 124, 133
Lewis, I. W. P., 43
Lewis, Winslow, 26, 27, 29, 31, 35, 36, 42
Lexington, Kentucky, 85
Life jackets, 74
Lifting device, 53 (see Holmes hoist)

Lifting jack, 54
Lighthouse board, 43, 45, 53, 73, 77
Lighthouse commissioner, 97
Lighthouse engineers, 16, 37, 60
Lighthouse keepers, 3, 19, 22, 29, 31, 34, 37,
    43, 45, 46, 47, 48, 53, 57, 58, 59, 63, 66,
    68, 69, 73, 74, 75, 76, 78, 79, 82, 83, 85,
    87, 91, 94, 95, 107, 109, 112, 114, 121,
    122, 131
Lighthouses, 13, 17, 18, 21, 23, 26, 27, 28,
    29, 32, 34, 35, 36, 40, 42, 43, 45, 47, 50,
    51, 52, 53, 54, 135
Lighthouse system, 15, 43, 45, 48
Lighting apparatus, 33
Lightning conductors, 70
Lights, 2, 15, 19, 21, 22, 24, 25, 28, 31, 39,
    49, 50, 55, 57, 59, 62
Lights out, 21
Lincoln, Abraham, 56
Lincoln, Levi, 36
List of duties, 12, 13
Little Brewster Island, 49
Loblolly Cove, 37, 69, 78, 79, 81, 82, 83, 92,
    101, 102, 103
"Lobster rock," 78
London, 3, 5
Londoner, 15, 16, 21, 23, 37, 46, 48, 49, 50,
    59, 67, 68, 74, 88, 89, 94
Lookout man, 122
*Lottie B.*, 74
Low, John, 13
Lowell, Massachusetts, 51, 52
Lynn, Massachusetts, 79

Mainland, 2, 17, 18, 25, 36, 38, 53, 57, 58,
    59, 62, 67, 69, 75, 76, 79, 83, 86, 87, 89,
    91, 92, 94, 98, 99, 100, 102, 105, 106, 107,
    108, 112, 119, 124, 126, 132
Maintenance, 23, 73, 122
Mantle of silk, 98, 110
Marblehead, 6, 10, 11, 13
*Margaret*, 25
Margeson, G. T., 102
Mariners, 6, 47, 55
*Marion*, 92
*Mary Sears*, 87

Massachusetts, 36, 49
Massachusetts Bay, 55
Massachusetts Bay Colony, 13, 17, 97
Massachusetts coast, 1
Massachusetts General Court, 3, 10, 13, 17,
    21, 22
Massachusetts Historical Commission, 119
Massachusetts Humane Society, 70, 74
Massachusetts State Guard Emergency
    Hospital, 88
Maverick, Moses, 5
*Mayflower*, 11
*Medford*, 67
Merrimack River, 51
*Meteor*, 31
Middlesex canal, 51
Milk Island, 40
Mills, Charles Edward, 83
Mills, Charles Frederick, 83
Mills, Edith, 75
Miniature national park, 132
Minot's light, 53, 84
Mitchell, John, 114
Mobile, Alabama, 52
Molasses truncheon, 54
Morris, June, 125
Mott, Elmo, 87, 88, 92

*Nancy*, 20
National Registry of Historic Places, 119, 120
Naval fleet, 70
Needham, Betty, 92

Needham, Hubert, 92, 100
New England, 5, 6, 10
New London, Connecticut, 42
New Sarum, 6
New towers, 49, 50, 57, 61
New Year's dinner, 91
*Nicanor*, 37
"Noah's Ark," 127
*Nodoc*, 83
Nor'easters, 2, 40, 58
North tower, 21, 44, 45, 55, 61, 62, 65, 68, 74, 77, 80, 88, 89, 91, 93, 96, 97, 98, 99, 100, 102, 111, 114, 116, 117, 118, 119, 120, 121, 122, 129, 134
Norton, Frederick (Chip), 129, 132
Notice to Mariners, 55

Oil containers, 2, 20, 25, 26, 59, 61, 62, 73
"Old and feeble," 28
Olson, Mildred Anderson, 48
One hundredth birthday, 66
Orders (sizes), 42, 45, 50, 51, 54, 97
Orne, Eleanor, 108
Orne, Geselle, 92
Orne, Simeon, 92, 94, 100, 104
Otis Air Force Base, 123
Oxen, 13, 16, 20, 51, 53

Painter, 47, 93
Painting, 48, 93, 102
Panes of glass, 22, 24, 26

Parabola, 27
Parrot, Laurie, 129
Parsons, Benjamin, Jr., 57
Parsons, Eleanor C., 57
Parsons, James Collins, 53, 57
Parsons, James C., Jr., 57
Parsons, Mary Ann, 57
Parsons, Raymond, 121
Pasturage, 13
Pea pod, 100
Pear tree, 13
Pebble beach, 37, 69
Pensacola, Florida, 52
Perley, Sydney, 51, 52
Perry, Matthew, 45
*Pierce*, 58
Pigeon Cove, 20, 29, 34, 35
Pigs, 92
Pinnace, 4, 5, 9
Pirate gold, 31
Pirates, 3
Piscataqua River, 4
Planted pears for his heirs, 11
Pleasonton, Stephen, 42, 43
Plummer, Samuel, 13
Plymouth, 11
Poison ivy, 101, 105, 107, 125
Political dissension, 29, 35, 79
Politicians, 15, 16, 71, 95
Pool, Ebenezer, 20, 31, 41, 58, 101
Poole, Ernest, 98, 120
Porch, 39, 72
Porter, Helen, 19
Portland Steam Packet Company, 47
Port pilots, 73
Portsmouth, 25
Post offices, 53
Potatoes, 28
Preservation, 121, 122
*President*, 41
Principal keepers, 25, 40, 59, 67, 74, 81, 85, 92, 93, 104
Prisoner of War, 59
Provincetown, 78
Provincial Congress, 18, 19
Public health nurse, 90
Public health services, 90, 91
Pulling Jack, 54
Purchase fall, 54

Quintals, 31
Quincy, 52
Quarries, 52, 54

Race Point, 78
Radio shack, 105
Railroad, 56, 72, 73, 79
Red Cross, 90
Reed, Alice, 78, 79
Reed, Louise, 78, 79
Reed, Richard, 13
Reed, William M., 77, 78, 79
Reef, 15, 48, 88 (see ledge)
Reflector, 25, 26, 27, 36, 45
Reinertsen, Edvardine, 84
Retirement Act, 74
Revolving lens, 16, 45
Rhode Island, 24
Robinson, Andrew, 4
Rock, 6, 9, 29, 37, 45, 48, 49, 50, 59, 74, 82, 83, 89, 112
Rock clearing, 29, 38
Rockport, 1, 36, 40, 48, 49, 52, 56, 57, 71, 79, 83, 85, 88, 111, 116, 118, 119, 120, 121, 122, 123
Rockport Granite Company, 71
Rowe, Belle Thacher, 48
Rowe, Lancelot Kelly, 47, 48, 57
Rowe, Nancy Beal, 48
Rowe, Sally, 22
Royal Tar, 37
Russia, 28

Salary, 17, 18, 59, 73, 74, 84, 85, 122, 123
Salem, 10, 23, 40, 52, 88
Salem Register, 52
Salvages, 50, 71
Sandy Bay Harbor, 5, 17, 20, 70, 71, 83
Sankety light, 84
Sargent, Winthrop, 34
Saunders, Douglas, 93, 104
Sayward, James, 28
Sayward, Joseph, 24, 25, 28, 132
Schedule of sailings, 4
School, 77, 78, 79, 81, 92
School houses, 53

Schooner, 4, 16, 34, 35, 37, 40, 41, 45, 54, 58, 67
Scientific experiments, 2, 25
Scottish coast, 27
Screamer, 71
Sea birds, 91
Sea gulls, 1, 91, 111, 118, 120, 126, 128, 135
Sea mosses, 59
Seasick, 106
Seavey, Cora, 92
Seavey, Emma, 92
Seavey, George, 92, 93, 94, 100, 104
Secretary of Commerce, 40
Secretary of Transportation, 119
Selection of lightkeeper, 122
Self-bailing boats, 74
Serving plate, 75
Sevo, 34, 35
Shaft, 49
Sheared wool, 102
Sheep and cattle, 17
Shipping interests, 13, 48
Shipwreck, 13, 59, 92
Shipwreck, earliest, 1
Signal of distress, 87
Silva, Everett (Snap), 106
"Silvered," 27
Site locations, 15, 16
Small basket, 37
Smith, Hoyt, 92
Smith, John, 3
Snakes, 82

Snow, Edward Rowe, 125
Snowstorms, 2, 61, 62
South Street, 81, 83
South tower, 21, 27, 42, 55, 61, 62, 68, 69,
  76, 79, 80, 81, 93, 97, 98, 99, 100, 104,
  109, 111, 114, 121, 122, 125, 134
Spanish American War, 68, 85
Spider lamp, 26, 27
Spiral staircase, 28, 61, 62
Spring on Thachers, 125
Standard apparel, 73
Standish, Myles, 11
Steam power, 54
St. John, New Brunswick, 74
Stone, 1, 50, 51, 52, 53, 54
Stone house, 30
Stone wall, 38, 39, 53
Storage closet, 63
Storm, 3, 5, 9, 31, 36, 37, 46, 49, 58, 61, 62,
  67, 71, 72, 75, 88, 91, 98, 100, 105, 109,
  129
Storm signal station, 67
Straitsmouth Island, 79, 87, 102
Strobe beam, 125
Sunday Blue Laws, 83
Superintendent of Lighthouses, 36
Supplies, 22
Survey, 95
Survivors, 59
Swenson quarries, 51
Swiss scientist, 25

Tarr, Addison Franklin, 69, 74, 77, 82, 83, 85
Tarr, Ed., 81
Tarr, Frederick H. (Ted), 120
Tarr, Mary Gilbert, 69, 92
Tarr, William H., 57
Telegraph, 67, 68
Telephone, 76, 94, 105, 124, 125, 126
Television, 108, 109
Temperature, 38
Thacher, Anthony, 3, 4, 5, 10, 11, 12, 13,
  17, 22, 101, 106, 121, 123, 135
Thacher, Bethia, 11
Thacher, Edith, 9
Thacher, Elizabeth Jones, 4, 5, 8, 11, 12, 17
Thacher, John, 11
Thacher, Judah, 11
Thacher, Mary, 8
Thacher, Peter (son of Anthony), 7, 9
Thacher, Peter (father of Thomas), 11
Thacher, Thomas, 11
Thacher, William, 9, 10
Thachers Island, 1, 13, 19, 21, 22, 23, 24, 25,
  26, 27, 28, 29, 31, 35, 36, 37, 38, 41, 42,
  45, 46, 47, 48, 49, 50, 51, 52, 54, 55, 56,
  57, 58, 59, 66, 68, 69, 70, 71, 72, 74, 75,
  77, 81, 82, 83, 84, 85, 86, 87, 89, 92, 93,
  98, 101, 102, 103, 104, 105, 109, 111, 112,
  114, 118, 125, 132, 135
Thachers Island Association, 132
Thacher's Woe, 3, 10
Thayer, James, 32
"The Congress," 20
Thibeault, Gene, 106
Thompson, 88
Thoreau, Henry David, 47, 76
Thunderstorms, 82
Tide, 5, 36, 49, 76, 105, 128, 132
Toothache, 114
Torys and patriots, 18
Totten, Joseph G., 53
Towle, Helen, 79, 82, 92
Towle, Henry C., 79, 82
Town appointed committee, 117, 121, 122,
  123, 124, 126, 127, 128, 129, 133
Town wharf, 83, 106, 133
Tracy, John Patrick, 13
Tragedies, 1, 2, 11, 75, 85, 135
Traitorous activities, 19

Transition years, 92
*Transport*, 35
Treasury, U. S., 21, 24, 25, 40
Tucker, William, 5
Tupper, Irving, 106
Turntable, 73
Turks' Heads, 3
Twin lights, 19, 20, 25, 27, 33, 45, 48, 49,
     50, 63, 66, 72, 94, 97, 98, 113, 114, 116
Twin sentinels, 20, 45, 76
Twin towers, 1, 16, 17, 29, 31, 32, 45, 49,
     51, 54, 55, 56, 63, 66, 68, 72, 77, 95, 100,
     116, 117, 120
Typhoid fever, 57, 85

Uniforms, 73, 84
United States, 42, 45, 84
United States Army, 53
United States Attorney General, 114
United States Board of Engineers, 71
United States Government, 1, 20, 23, 24, 26,
     27, 28, 29, 39, 43, 53, 68, 83, 95, 97, 98,
     115, 118, 119
United States Marshalls, 113
United States Navy, 83
University of Maine, 132
Unwelcome guest, 112

Vandals, 21
Veator, J., 120
Vessels, 20, 31, 34, 36, 37, 45, 54, 56, 58, 66,
     68, 70, 75, 83, 94, 102
Volpe, John, 119

Walen, Harry, 121
Walkway, 64, 88
War of 1812, 27
Washington, D. C., 42, 71
Washington, George, 20, 25
Watch, 40
*Watch and Wait*, 3, 37, 135
Water pollution, 73
Weather, 3, 38, 49, 54, 63, 67, 81, 82, 90,
     91, 92, 124, 125

West coast lightkeepers, 41
Westford quarries, 51
Whale oil lamps, 25
Whale watching, 76
Wheeler, Aaron, 29, 31, 33, 34, 37, 41, 53
Wheeler, Austin, 34
Wheeler, Charles, 34, 36, 37, 38, 39, 41, 42,
     53, 59, 101
Wheeler, John, 34
Wheeler, Moses, 34
Wherry, 40
Whig, 40
Whitaker, Bertha Whitten, 74, 75
Whitaker, Harold, 75, 131
Whitaker, Sylvia, 75
White, John, 13
Whittemore, Samuel, 21
Whitten, Albert L., 74, 75, 76
Wicks, 20, 25, 26, 43, 59, 97
Wilbur, Harry A., 93, 104
Wild strawberries, 78
Williams, Victor, 106
Wilson, Thomas Woodrow, 85, 88, 89
Workdays, 127
World War I, 87
World War II, 105, 108
W. P. A. Program, 94
Wrecked vessel, 3, 37, 92, 135

Yankee, 43
Yarmouth, Massachusetts, 11

# THACHERS

*has been published in a first edition*
*of two thousand sewn, softcover copies.*
*Designed by A. L. Morris,*
*the text was composed in Paladium*
*and printed by Sherwin/Dodge, Printers*
*in Littleton, New Hampshire on Mohawk Vellum.*
*The binding was executed by New Hampshire Bindery*
*in Concord, New Hampshire.*